UNDERSTANDING
DAVID MAMET

UNDERSTANDING CONTEMPORARY AMERICAN LITERATURE
Matthew J. Bruccoli, Founding Editor
Linda Wagner-Martin, Series Editor

Volumes on

Edward Albee | Sherman Alexie | Nelson Algren | Paul Auster
Nicholson Baker | John Barth | Donald Barthelme | The Beats
Thomas Berger | The Black Mountain Poets | Robert Bly
T. C. Boyle | Raymond Carver | Fred Chappell | Chicano Literature
Contemporary American Drama | Contemporary American Horror Fiction
Contemporary American Literary Theory
Contemporary American Science Fiction, 1926–1970
Contemporary American Science Fiction, 1970–2000
Contemporary Chicana Literature | Robert Coover | Philip K. Dick
James Dickey | E. L. Doctorow | Rita Dove | John Gardner | George Garrett
Tim Gautreaux | John Hawkes | Joseph Heller | Lillian Hellman | Beth Henley
John Irving | Randall Jarrell | Charles Johnson | Adrienne Kennedy
William Kennedy | Jack Kerouac | Jamaica Kincaid | Tony Kushner
Ursula K. Le Guin | Denise Levertov | Bernard Malamud | David Mamet
Bobbie Ann Mason | Colum McCann | Cormac McCarthy | Jill McCorkle
Carson McCullers | W. S. Merwin | Arthur Miller | Lorrie Moore
Toni Morrison's Fiction | Vladimir Nabokov | Gloria Naylor
Joyce Carol Oates | Tim O'Brien | Flannery O'Connor | Cynthia Ozick
Walker Percy | Katherine Anne Porter | Richard Powers | Reynolds Price
Annie Proulx | Thomas Pynchon | Theodore Roethke | Philip Roth
May Sarton | Hubert Selby, Jr. | Mary Lee Settle | Neil Simon
Isaac Bashevis Singer | Jane Smiley | Gary Snyder | William Stafford
Robert Stone | Anne Tyler | Gerald Vizenor | Kurt Vonnegut
David Foster Wallace | Robert Penn Warren | James Welch | Eudora Welty
Tennessee Williams | August Wilson | Charles Wright

UNDERSTANDING

DAVID MAMET

Brenda Murphy

The University of South Carolina Press

© 2011 University of South Carolina

Published by the University of South Carolina Press
Columbia, South Carolina 29208

www.sc.edu/uscpress

Manufactured in the United States of America

20 19 18 17 16 15 14 13 12 11   10 9 8 7 6 5 4 3 2 1

Library of Congress Cataloging-in-Publication Data

Murphy, Brenda, 1950–
    Understanding David Mamet / Brenda Murphy.
        p. cm. — (Understanding contemporary American literature)
    Includes bibliographical references and index.
    ISBN 978-1-61117-002-3 (cloth : alk. paper)
    1. Mamet, David—Criticism and interpretation. I. Title.
    PS3563.A4345Z8 2011
    812'.54—dc22

                                                            2011010283

This book was printed on Glatfelter Natures, a recycled paper with 30 percent
postconsumer waste content.

*To my parents, Phil and Priscilla Murphy, and my sisters
and brothers, Bill, Claire, Bob, Rich, and Pat, with
cherished memories of a Chicagoland childhood*

CONTENTS

Series Editors' Preface *ix*

Chapter 1
Understanding David Mamet *1*

Chapter 2
The Essays *11*

Chapter 3
Men with Men, Women with Women *22*

Chapter 4
Men and Women *44*

Chapter 5
Parents and Children *59*

Chapter 6
Confidence Games *69*

Chapter 7
Degeneration and Descent *89*

Chapter 8
The Novels *108*

Notes *123*
Bibliography *133*
Index *139*

SERIES EDITORS' PREFACE

The volumes of *Understanding Contemporary American Literature* have been planned as guides or companions for students as well as good nonacademic readers. The editors and publisher perceive a need for these books because much influential contemporary literature makes special demands. Literature relies on conventions, but conventions keep evolving; new writers form their own conventions—which in time may become familiar.

The word *understanding* in the titles was chosen deliberately. Many willing readers lack an adequate understanding of how contemporary literature works; that is, of what the author is attempting to express. Although the criticism and analysis in the series have been aimed at a level of general accessibility, these introductory volumes are meant to be applied in conjunction with the works they cover.

Matthew J. Bruccoli, Founding Editor

A decade into the twenty-first century, Professor Bruccoli's prescience gives us an avenue to publish expert critiques of significant contemporary American writing. The series continues to map the literary landscape and to provide both instruction and enjoyment.

Linda Wagner-Martin, Series Editor

CHAPTER 1

Understanding David Mamet

Understanding David Mamet is no mean feat. As his friend and collaborator of forty years, William H. Macy, told an interviewer, "He's an easy man to know a little [. . .] he's a difficult man to know well."[1] Born in 1947, Mamet has been in the public eye since the 1970s, when his success with *Sexual Perversity in Chicago* (1974) and *American Buffalo* (1975) turned him into the theater's boy genius from Chicago. In the decades since, the public has been treated to a series of David Mamet personae, decked out in a series of suitable costumes. In 1977 the twenty-nine-year-old Mamet was described by an interviewer as "looking as respectable as an assistant librarian" and "precisely the type of young man that corporate executives and university faculty love to write references for. He is young, bright and personable. Neat, sober and responsible. Honest, alert and probably dozens of other virtuous things as well."[2] It was hard to imagine that Mamet had been "the author of the foulest language on Broadway" in *American Buffalo*. A photograph shows an earnest Mamet with a stylish modified shag haircut and large glasses with clear plastic frames, wearing a neutral sweater with a scarf wrapped casually around his neck. Another interview from the same period describes him as "chunkily built and button-bright-eyed" with "a certain post-academic puppy-dog charm."[3] The photographs with this piece show a tousle-headed Mamet without glasses and in a dark pullover, jeans, and sandals.

In his younger days Mamet was voluble and enthusiastic in interviews, and a number of interviewers noticed his curious style of conversation, the tough-guy street talk of Chicago blending with multisyllabic words and references to his voluminous reading that ranged from Aristotle and Epictetus to Veblen and Tolstoy to Stanislavsky, Meyerhold, and Brecht. "David Mamet isn't afraid of words; he makes you believe that words are afraid of him. They

come pouring out of his mouth the same way they stream through his pen—
in perfect rhythm,"[4] wrote one interviewer. As Mamet grew older and experienced some of the not-so-welcome side effects of fame, however, he became
more circumspect. In 1984 an interview preceding the production of *Glengarry Glen Ross* described his manner as "coiled, caustic, funny, slightly
guarded."[5] In the years that followed, a Mamet interview increasingly became
a contest between an interviewer trying to wrest information or opinions out
of him and a writer who evaded questions with monosyllabic answers, jokes,
tangential lectures, or questions of his own.

In the early nineties, after Mamet wrote some startlingly revelatory essays
about his difficult childhood, his manner in interviews became even more
closed. One interviewer commented that "it's hard to know many things for
sure about David Mamet because Mamet works hard at being unknowable."[6] Yet, even now, Mamet continues to give interviews, partly because,
as playwright, director, and filmmaker, it is necessary to his job, and perhaps
partly because he enjoys the performance and the contest. In 1999 the
British reporter Andrew Billen, who was interviewing Mamet "with the non-
confrontational purpose of celebrating *The Winslow Boy*," Mamet's film
adaptation of Terrence Rattigan's play, soon found himself in an interview
"with David Mamet, Chicago's native bard of lies, deceit and aggression.
Mamet believes interviewers merely pose as honest truth-seekers and are
actually there to catch him out." Although "superficially polite," Mamet,
dressed "in his usual combat uniform of black shirt, black beard and black
crew cut [. . .] likes getting his retaliation in first."[7] When Mamet began the
interview with stories about men dueling with Bowie knives, Billen realized
that "while I am content to do my best, this is an interview Mamet wants to
win."[8] Mamet won.

The classic image of Mamet from the 1990s and early 2000s is that of the
film director in baseball cap, signature large, round, dark glasses, short beard,
and casual clothes that suggest his beloved Vermont woods. In 2000 a Canadian reporter said that, although "his behaviour with strangers is polite, unas-
suming and almost courtly," a conversation with him "is like trying to lure a
wolf away from guarding its pup. He'll pace back and forth, watching for a
moment of weakness, but he won't lunge until he feels he or his territory is
threatened."[9] In the same year, a British reporter was surprised to find Mamet
in a "cheery and affable mood" when he met him, but when they started to
discuss his novel *Wilson*, "cheery-normal Mamet suddenly turns into odd,
threateningly-playful Mamet, intent on coating each answer with a layer of
comic strangeness and turning the interview into something akin to performance art."[10] In 2002 Mamet moved with his wife, Rebecca Pidgeon, and their

two children from Newton, Massachusetts, and Cabot, Vermont, to Santa Monica, and he seemed to have undergone another sea change. Although he has not exactly "gone Hollywood," Mamet, who produced his own television show, *The Unit,* from 2006 to 2010, has shed the backwoods look for more California-friendly clothes, favors a beret, often worn backwards, over a cap, and is occasionally seen in a jacket and tie. In his early sixties he does not seem to be through with his evolving persona. Over the years he has given thoughtful, straightforward statements about his work and ideas in interviews with academics and critics who show a serious interest in his work rather than curiosity about his life, and decades of study and criticism have yielded many insights into his plays and other writings. Still we are far from understanding David Mamet.

Interestingly, while revealing little about his inner life, in his eleven volumes of essays and the many interviews he has granted over forty years, Mamet has left a good record of the bare facts. He was born David Allen Mamet on 30 November 1947 in Flossmoor, Illinois, a suburb of Chicago. His father, Bernard, was a successful labor lawyer, his mother, Lenore (Lee) Silver Mamet, had been a special education teacher. All four of his grandparents were Ashkenazi Jews from within two hundred miles of Warsaw. When David was two years old, the family moved to Chicago's South Side, settling on the edge of a Jewish neighborhood near Hyde Park and the University of Chicago. His sister, Lynn, was born in 1950, and the two have always been close, most recently working on the television show *The Unit* together. Mamet has fond memories of growing up on the South Side, although he has come to think that the religious training he received at the liberal Temple Sinai was too assimilationist, undermining his sense of Jewish identity. The elder Mamets' marriage was difficult, ending, according to biographer Ira Nadel, in two incidents of physical violence.[11] They were divorced in April 1959, when David was eleven years old, and three days later Lee Mamet married Bernard Kleiman, another lawyer who had worked with Bernard Mamet.

Bernard and Lee Kleiman bought a house in a new subdivision in the southwest Chicago suburb of Olympia Fields, where they lived with David and Lynn; Kleiman's two children, David and Leslie, visited on weekends. As revealed in Mamet's personal essay, "The Rake," and his avowedly autobiographical play, *Jolly,* the new family was deeply dysfunctional with the children, particularly Lynn, subjected to both physical and emotional abuse. David miserably attended schools that he hated. When he was fourteen, he left that summer to live on Chicago's North Side with his father and his new family, including two stepbrothers, Tony, who became an actor and appears in several of David's films, and Bobby, who became a musician. David, who was not doing well academically, was sent to the progressive Francis Parker School, which did not have grades and focused on individual learning. He flourished there, studied the piano, and enjoyed forays around the city, hanging out in pool halls, hustling Ping-Pong, playing poker, going to film festivals, and haunting the stores on Wabash Avenue. Although he has belittled the education he got at Goddard College in Vermont, particularly in an essay titled "Sex Camp," he has acknowledged that his academic record was such that he was lucky to be admitted, and the college's unregimented academic program, which allowed students to pursue their own individual interests, was similar to the atmosphere of Francis Parker. As a boy Mamet had acted in television productions by the Chicago Board of Rabbis, and in high school he had worked at menial jobs in several Chicago theaters, including the improv troupe Second City. He reveled in the sense of being part of the theater. It was at Goddard, however, that his enthusiasm gelled into an ambition to make the theater his career. He spent his junior year studying acting at the Neighborhood Playhouse in New York and working backstage at the off-Broadway phenomenon *The Fantasticks*, and his senior project at Goddard was his first produced play, a Second City–style dramatic piece in thirty-four scenes, CAMEL / *A Review by David Mamet*.

After his graduation from Goddard in 1969, Mamet acted for a while in Montreal and then returned to Chicago, where he lived in a room in the Lincoln Hotel, near Francis Parker School and the Lincoln Park Zoo, relishing his view of Lake Michigan and the park, where he often sat on a bench writing. It was here that *The Duck Variations* (1972), dialogues between two elderly men sitting on a park bench, was conceived. During this time Mamet worked in the "boiler room" of a real estate office, generating leads for the salesmen, who would then go out and close the deals. He drew on this experience for *Glengarry Glen Ross* (1983). In 1970 and 1971 he taught acting at Marlboro College and at Goddard, where he taught William H. Macy and Steven Schachter, with whom he formed the St. Nicholas Theater Company, with Mamet as artistic director. When Mamet returned to Chicago in 1972, they, along with Patricia Cox, reconstituted the company there, and it soon became a significant part of the new off-Loop theater movement, producing Mamet's plays among others. It was at this time that Mamet had his first success as a playwright, with his plays performed in various Chicago theaters, notably *Sexual Perversity in Chicago* (1974), his comedy about the lives of young Chicago singles, at the Organic Theatre, and *American Buffalo* (1975), his tragedy about the corruption of love and friendship by the pursuit of money among three men living on the margins of urban society, at the Goodman, Chicago's most prestigious theater.

In 1975 an off-Broadway production of *Sexual Perversity* and *Duck Variations* won him an Obie for best play. In 1976 he resigned as artistic director of the St. Nicholas and moved to New York, where he lived in Chelsea, a neighborhood that reminded him of Chicago. *American Buffalo* opened on Broadway in 1977, marking Mamet's arrival as a major American playwright and establishing his reputation as a genius of "foul-mouthed" dialogue. That year also saw productions of *All Men Are Whores, A Life in the Theatre, The Water Engine, Reunion, Dark Pony, The Woods,* and two children's plays, *The Revenge of the Space Pandas, or Binky Rudich* and *The Two-Speed Clock.* The reception accorded these plays was mixed, but Mamet at the age of thirty had become an established playwright whose plays were being produced in both New York and Chicago's Goodman Theatre as well as other major regional theaters. *Sexual Perversity* and *Duck Variations* were also produced in London that year.

The year 1977 was also important to Mamet for his marriage to the actress Lindsay Crouse. The daughter of playwright Russell Crouse, who, with Howard Lindsay, wrote some of the most successful plays in American theater history, including *Life with Father, State of the Union,* and *The Sound of Music,* Crouse grew up in a Park Avenue apartment surrounded by Broadway royalty. Mamet pursued her intensely, having, he said, fallen in love with her when he saw her in the movie *Slap Shot,* and going to New Haven expressly to meet her when she was in the Yale Repertory Theatre production of his *Reunion.* They were married in her mother's apartment on 21 December 1977 and both rising stars were often interviewed together during the early years of their marriage. Crouse quickly joined what has come to be known as the "Mamet mafia," the close group of actors and other theater and film artists who regularly work in his productions and films and function for him as an artistic family. With her help he was hired to write the script for *The Verdict* (1982), which won him an Oscar nomination, and she headed the cast of Mamet veterans in the first film he wrote and directed, *House of Games* (1987). In 1978 they bought the farm house with one hundred acres in Cabot, Vermont, that was to feed Mamet's imagination in writing his novel *The Village* (1994) and his film *State and Main* (2000) as well as many essays. Shortly after they bought the house, Crouse made Mamet the gift of a small "writing cabin" near the house, where he was to write a good deal of his work. They have two daughters, Willa, a photographer, and Zosia, an actor. Mamet and Crouse were divorced in 1990.

The mid-1970s had truly seen a meteoric rise for Mamet, and his career perhaps inevitably cooled off a bit in the next few years. Audiences and critics were somewhat bewildered by some of the turns his playwriting took, most especially his exercise in lyrical mythmaking, *The Lone Canoe* (1979). This play, a historical musical based on a short story by Jack London, is about a British explorer lost in the wilds of Michigan's Upper Peninsula. Its premiere, which unfortunately took place before the Society of American Theatre Critics, was panned far and wide. The year 1979 also saw the New York production of the intense and symbolic drama of a love relationship, *The Woods*. This play is in some sense the tragedy that is latent in the comedy of *Sexual Perversity in Chicago*. Mamet has counted it among the four plays he calls classical tragedies, and he has said that he originally composed it in verse. Rooted in what Mamet has called the "symbology" of dream and fairy tale and owing a good deal to Anton Chekhov and Ernest Hemingway in style, it is his most complex dramatization of the profound difficulty of honest communication between human beings, particularly men and women. It was received respectfully, but not enthusiastically, by the critics, and it was not a financial or popular success.

Lakeboat, produced in 1982 at the Goodman and at Long Wharf in New Haven, is an intensely personal play written just after Mamet's graduation from Goddard College and based on his then-recent experience of working for a summer on an ore boat on the Great Lakes. It was first produced in 1970 at Marlboro College, while Mamet was teaching there. He later described it as one of his "feeling slices of interesting life [. . .] episodic glimpses of humanity."[12] The play is a series of twenty-eight brief scenes, some less than a page of dialogue, dramatizing the interaction among the sailors on the lakeboat *T. Harrison.* It is also an exploration of the meaning and use of narrative within this community. Perhaps because of its fondly nostalgic tone, it has never been as well received as Mamet's edgier plays about male communities.

During the early 1980s Mamet came back with a vengeance, producing some of the best and most successful works of the kind that audiences and critics expected him to write. He began what would be a long career in filmmaking with the screenplays for *The Postman Always Rings Twice* (1981) and *The Verdict.* In 1982 he won an Obie for the Goodman Theatre's production of *Edmond,* and he achieved his greatest success in the theater to date with *Glengarry Glen Ross,* which ran for 378 performances on Broadway and won a number of awards, including the Pulitzer Prize for Drama. *Glengarry* solidified Mamet's reputation as the playwright of the hard-boiled world of men and the creator of what has come to be known as "Mametspeak" in the theater, dialogue that reflects Mamet's idea that conversation is not only speech act but combat, that each character is always using speech to get something from the others or to win in the constant struggle for dominance. Although it is carefully crafted and rhythmic, his dialogue gives the impression of ragged vernacular speech, with its fragmented sentences, stutters, ellipses, repetitions, staccato rhythms, and, most famously, expletives. Mamet's unique effect often comes from the juxtaposition of a curiously formal diction with blunt or vernacular language: "What you're hired for is to *help* us—does that seem clear to you? To *help* us. *Not* to fuck us up . . . to help *men* who are going *out* there to try to earn a *living*. You *fairy*. You company man."[13] Mamet's dialogue has been imitated by a generation of young playwrights, but it remains unique in the theater. As he told an interviewer, "the dialogue of my plays, as one might assume, is the result of a great gift which I was, I guess, born with, and a great deal of work, which I did pay for. It really has nothing to do with writing down things you hear on a bus."[14]

The success of *Glengarry Glen Ross* was followed by that of the 1988 Tony Award–winning *Speed-the-Plow*, which, partly owing to the presence of Madonna in a lead role, ran for 279 performances on Broadway. Mamet's iconoclastic representation of the movie business is similar to his depiction of the real estate business in *Glengarry Glen Ross*, and he received similar accolades for it. In the meantime, however, he adapted three of Chekhov's plays, *The Cherry Orchard*, *Uncle Vanya*, and *Three Sisters*, and the short story *Vint*, and he wrote two haunting works of his own, *Prairie du Chien* and *The Shawl*, none of which would be considered "hard boiled." While the characteristic rhythms are there, as well as the ellipses and the broken sentences (which Mamet partly learned from Chekhov), these plays show the range of which Mamet is capable. Written as a radio play, *Prairie du Chien* takes place on a train in 1910. Accompanied by the background sounds of a game of gin rummy, it is driven by the gruesome and haunting story one man tells another about a woman whose spirit directed would-be rescuers to her lover's body after her husband had killed them and himself. In *The Shawl* a small-time charlatan psychic evinces humane principles despite making his living by defrauding vulnerable clients.

During this period Mamet also wrote the screenplays for *The Untouchables* (1987), *House of Games* (1987), and *We're No Angels* (1990), three quite different films. *The Untouchables*, the story of Elliot Ness's crusade against Al Capone, contains what are probably Mamet's most famous film lines, spoken by Jimmy Malone (Sean Connery) as the Chicago cop who teaches Ness how to deal with Chicago gangs: "You wanna know how to get Capone? They pull a knife, you pull a gun. He sends one of yours to the hospital, you send one of his to the morgue. *That*'s the *Chicago* way!" *House of Games*, the first film that Mamet wrote and directed himself, is a psychological suspense film about a subject that has been of enduring interest to him, confidence men and con games. The remake of the 1955 Michael Curtiz film

We're No Angels features Sean Penn and Robert de Niro cast against type in a sweet comedy about two escaped convicts who find a haven among the inhabitants of a small village when they are mistaken for two priests.

In 1991 Mamet married Rebecca Pidgeon, whom he had met when she acted in the London production of *Speed-the-Plow*. Eighteen years younger than Mamet and trained at the Royal Academy of Dramatic Arts, Pidgeon had a dual career as an actress and the lead singer of the group Ruby Blue before her marriage. Afterward she began to focus on acting and became a central member of the "Mamet mafia," along with Joe Mantegna, J. J. Johnston, Colin Stinton, Tony Mamet, Linda Kimbrough, Ricky Jay, and close friends William H. Macy and Felicity Huffman, who have a house near Mamet's in Vermont. Pidgeon appeared in *Homicide* (1991), a film about a detective who is forced to confront his feelings about his Jewish identity, which Mamet wrote and directed, and she acted opposite Macy in *Oleanna* (1992), perhaps the most controversial of Mamet's plays as a result of its treatment of the hot-button issue of sexual harassment in an academic setting and of its ending, in which the male character beats the female character. Because she was pregnant at the time, Pidgeon did not appear in Mamet's film adaptation of *Oleanna* (1994), although she did the musical score for it. She did, however, appear in his films *The Spanish Prisoner* (1997), *The Winslow Boy* (1999), *State and Main* (2000), *Heist* (2001), *Edmond* (2005), and *Redbelt* (2008), and she had a recurring role in his television series, *The Unit*. Mamet and Pidgeon have a daughter, Clara, and a son, Noah.

In the 1990s Mamet engaged in an intense reexamination of his relationship to Judaism and his Jewish identity. Rebecca Pidgeon converted to Judaism before their marriage, and together they studied with several rabbis. Following the film *Homicide,* Mamet produced a series of works that reflected his new passion, including *The Old Religion* (1997), *The Old Neighborhood* (1997), and, most notably, *The Wicked Son: Anti-Semitism, Self-Hatred, and the Jews* (2006), a series of thirty-seven short pieces addressed to the assimilated or "fallen-away" Jew whom Mamet exhorts, in no uncertain terms, to come back to the fold. *The Old Religion* is based on a historical event, the 1914 case of Leo Max Frank, a southern Jew who was falsely accused of murdering one of the female workers in his textile factory and was convicted, kidnaped from prison, and lynched. A series of meditations in the mind of Frank as the trial progresses, it is closer to a modernist experiment in narrative subjectivity than to a typical historical novel. *The Old Neighborhood* consists of three short plays, *The Disappearance of the Jews, Jolly,* and *Deeny,* each of which has a strong autobiographical element. In the first one Bobby has come back to his old Chicago neighborhood from Los Angeles and has a conversation with his old friend Joey about their youth and their general feeling of being cut off from their Jewish roots. Bobby is a name Mamet uses in several plays, including *Bobby Gould in Hell* (1989), for autobiographical characters. The second, the most autobiographical play Mamet has written, is a conversation between Bobby and his sister Jolly about their relationship, their abusive childhood, and its effect on them as adults. The third is an elusive conversation between Bobby and a woman who had been his high school sweetheart.

According to his friends and relatives, Mamet's marriage to Rebecca Pidgeon had a calming effect on the man his sister, Lynn, called "the angriest man who was ever born"; his wife commented that "life has gotten a bit easier for him lately."[15] It was after his second marriage that Mamet began to reexamine in his writing some of the sources of his anger, particularly those in his childhood. Lynn Mamet has said, "suffice it to say we are not the victims of a happy childhood [. . .] there was a lot of violence, but the greatest violence was emotional. It was emotional terrorism. In my estimation, we are survivors of a travel route that included a 1950's version of Dachau and Bergen-Belsen, and that we both still bear the numbers on our arms. In that sense, when he writes, he wears short sleeves." She was quite sure that the origin of the rage in his plays is "all familial."[16] In *The Cabin* (1992), which is dedicated to Lynn, Mamet published several essays about his family and his childhood, including "The Watch," about his relationship with his father, and the startlingly revealing essay "The Rake," which gives some of the details of the physical abuse and "emotional terrorism" that Lynn referred to. *Jolly*, the second of the three plays in *The Old Neighborhood*, tells the story from the sister's point of view. "It was as if David had replayed six or eight of our phone conversations," said Lynn.[17] The literary culmination of this reexamination of the family is *The Cryptogram* (1994), a play which has "the dynamics of a soul murder," in John Lahr's memorable formulation.[18] Its subjects are the fruitless struggle of a ten-year-old boy to understand the unfathomable words and actions of the self-absorbed adults around him as his parents' marriage is breaking up and their obliviousness to the state of his fragile psyche as he confronts a world that has suddenly slipped its moorings.

At the end of the 1990s, another sea change was apparent, as Mamet wrote and directed *State and Main* (1999), simultaneously a lightly satirical comedy about the movie business and a fond treatment of the village life of Cabot, Vermont, that he had known for twenty years. More surprising was *Boston Marriage* (1999), a play he wrote for Rebecca Pidgeon and Felicity

Huffman. Something of an answer to critics who had consistently said that Mamet could not write women characters and to the accusations of misogyny that had followed *Oleanna,* this witty comedy of manners written in the style of Oscar Wilde concerns a lesbian couple whose romantic relationship triumphs, to a degree, over mercenary motives. Although it is imbued with the spirit of postmodernism, his 2001 sui generis work *Wilson* is a postapocalyptic novel in which the apocalypse is the crash of the Internet. In one sense the book is a 336-page joke on academic scholars who try to generalize about civilization from the odd fragments they focus on; in another it is an extended meditation on the decline of civilization and the impossibility of arriving at a viable sense of truth. This was followed in 2006 by his book of cartoons, *Tested on Orphans,* and in 2007 by his play *November,* a broadly comic satire of the U.S. political system. Clearly a less angry, more playfully imaginative David Mamet has emerged in the twenty-first century.

Not that the angry Mamet is gone. He is clearly evident in *The Wicked Son,* in which he excoriates his fellow Jews who have turned their back on their religion or who fail to support the state of Israel. But there is a new note of humor in his political and social writing. The 2008 essay "Why I Am No Longer a Brain-Dead Liberal," in which he announced that he had changed his mind about politics and was now reading with approval the likes of Thomas Sowell and Milton Friedman, is not a diatribe, but a humorous and, for Mamet, self-deprecating statement of how he has come to change his mind. The 2009 play *Race,* which raises the same kinds of uncomfortable questions about the race issue in contemporary life as *Oleanna* had about sexual harassment in the 1990s, is less relentlessly confrontational, accomplishing a good deal through humor.

What Mamet will we see next? The writer who called out his fellow Jews "whose favorite Jew is Anne Frank and whose second-favorite does not exist"[19] is writing and directing a movie about Anne Frank for Walt Disney Productions. Since 2008 he has shown a renewed interest in Broadway productions of his plays, with revivals of *American Buffalo, Speed-the-Plow, A Life in the Theater,* and *Oleanna,* and the new plays *Race,* which he directed, and *November.* Mamet's television show *The Unit,* which was cancelled by CBS in 2009 after four seasons, was quickly syndicated by Fox, which should bring Mamet a healthy sum. At the age of sixty-two, he is at a high point of productivity and professional recognition, not to mention finances. That may be a sign that something new is coming. Whatever it is, it will probably add another complication to understanding David Mamet.

CHAPTER 2

The Essays

Mamet has written eleven volumes of essays, and there are more that remain uncollected from magazines. Although his range is wide, particularly as he takes in American popular culture, some major topics recur often. As will be noted from titles such as *True and False: Heresy and Common Sense for the Actor* (1997), *Three Uses of the Knife: On the Nature and Purpose of Drama* (1998), *On Directing Film* (1991), *Bambi vs. Godzilla: On the Nature, Purpose, and Practice of the Movie Business* (2007), and *Theatre* (2010), theater and film are perennial preoccupations. In other collections, such as *Writing in Restaurants* (1986), *Some Freaks* (1989), *The Cabin* (1992), *Make-Believe Town* (1996), *Jafsie and John Henry* (1999), *South of the Northeast Kingdom* (2002), and *The Wicked Son: Anti-Semitism, Self Hatred, and the Jews* (2006), he writes about a wide variety of subjects from intimate family memoirs to personal essays on his feelings about such things as poker games, knife collecting, hunting, comic books, and public radio, to controversial opinion pieces on religion, ethnicity, and politics.

In the Company of Men

Most characteristic of the persona that David Mamet presents to the world are the essays on the joys of poker and other traditionally "masculine" pleasures such as the pool hall, the gun show, cigars, hunting, and knives. Dating back to the 1980s, these essays probably proceeded partly from Mamet's contrarian streak. As he wrote in *Some Freaks*, "in my quite misguided youth, I believed what the quite misguided women of my age said when they told me and my fellows that what was required for a Happy Union was a man who was, in all things, save plumbing, more or less a woman."[1] During the 1980s, he asserted, he took it upon himself to speak up for what he called "That Fun Which Dare Not Speak Its Name [. . .]" which has been given the unhappy tag 'male bonding'" (87). He wrote that there are three things for which men get together: doing business, bitching about women, and "hanging out," that is, "spending time with the boys," which he is loathe to call "bonding." He describes an ideal "Male Society," an environment where "one is understood, where one is not judged, where one is not expected to perform—because there is room in Male Society for the novice and the expert; room for all, in the Poker Game, the Golf Outing, the Sunday Watching Football; and room and encouragement for all who wholeheartedly endorse the worth of the activity" (88). This, he says, is the true benefit of being in the "Company of Men," which operates by the adage, "You will be greeted on the basis of your actions: no one will inquire into your sincerity, your history, or your views. If you do not choose to share them. We, the men, are here engaged in this specific activity, and your willingness to participate in the effort of the group will admit you." He admits that "yes, these activities are a form of love" (89). He also describes this male companionship, though it seems to be based in competition or the passing of money back and forth, as a "quest for grace," not for a mythical grace or for its "specious limitations," but for "an experience of *true* grace, and transcendent of the rational, and, so, more approximate to the real nature of the world" (90).

It is perhaps no surprise that this essay first appeared in *Playboy* magazine, but Mamet was staking out a serious position in the much-contested "post-feminist" culture of the late twentieth century. His views were not unlike those of one of his heroes, Ernest Hemingway, in the 1920s, but he felt himself to be writing as a battle-scarred veteran of a feminist period, the 1970s, defending the rights of men to preserve their own pursuits and institutions from disappearing amid the "feminization" of U.S. culture. Although this feminization might be translated as his wife's resistance to his smoking cigars in the house and playing in a weekly high-stakes poker game, he felt a need to preserve what he felt was the unique experience of being among men engaged in "male" pursuits.

Mamet was certainly eloquent in describing his pleasure in these activities, each of which seemed to have some unique quality for him. In "Pool Halls," collected in his first volume of prose, *Writing in Restaurants,* he explained how hanging out in the old Chicago pool halls in his youth taught him the joy of solitude, of being alone among men: "People are supposed to gamble here, people are supposed to drink here, people are supposed to spend their days here in pursuit of skill, cunning, comradeship, and money. No one is supposed to be pompous here, or intrusive, or boring [. . .] but if they choose, they can choose to be left alone."[2] In several essays over the years, Mamet has explained what he learned from playing in a decades-long poker game in Vermont and, most memorably in "Six Hours of Perfect Poker" in *Jafsie and John Henry*, what led him to stop playing. Some of his best prose is devoted to hunting and the experience of being in the outdoors in northern New England. He never actually describes killing an animal while hunting, but there is a sense that getting the deer is not what it is really about. Instead it is about nature and learning and the company of other men. "What an education one can get out in the woods," he wrote, "the wind, the weather, the food sources, and the phases of the moon, the habits of deer, and of the other animals [. . .] are all part of the study," and, at the end of even a failed hunting season, a nostalgic review "seems to banish remorse and to goad information into knowledge, and to gently counsel thanks."[3]

Mamet always presents himself as something of a schlemiel in the woods, the perennial city boy who learns much of his outdoors lore out of books and will never be one of the native hunters he so admires, no matter how much he learns from them. But it is in "Late Season Hunt" in *Jafsie and John Henry* that he seems best to understand and accept his true relation to the woods and hunting. After a fall season of living in New York, where all he hunts is a short line for gourmet coffee, he takes the occasion of his fiftieth birthday to take a quick trip to Vermont for the end of the hunting season. His weekend in the woods with two expert hunters leaves him physically exhausted and, of course, without a deer, but sleeping well, and he decides that "it was not a bad performance for a dissipated city fellow with a desk job."[4] As usual he has brought too much gear, his rifle falls apart, and he sweats through his clothes and gets so cold that he has to buy new ones when they stop for lunch, but he ends the essay with an observation that shows his study of the woods has led to some self-knowledge: "As a hunter, of course, I am a fraud. But it was a hell of a good vacation" (171).

Autobiography

Mamet writes less about women than about men, but he has written some memorable essays focused particularly on his mother and his sister. He has written the occasional diatribe about male-female relationships, but perhaps the most notorious of his essays about women is "True Stories of Bitches" in *Writing in Restaurants*. This essay has often been used as proof of his misogyny because of its explanation of the "*raison d'être* of bitchiness and its identification as a feminine tactic." In the essay he defined bitchiness as the "ne plus ultra of response," and he suggested, "We've all got to have an ace in the hole when dealing with those who are stronger" (44). His explanation for the way this works is in husband-and-wife arguments when "the ultimate response the man feels is, of course, physical violence. People can say what they will, we men think, but if I get pushed just one little step further, why I might, I might just _____ (FILL IN THE BLANK) because she seems to have forgotten that I'M STRONGER THAN HER" (44). This statement has been quoted, particularly in relation to *Oleanna,* as an endorsement of male violence, but it is clear in the context of the essay that that is not what Mamet intended at all. The point of the essay is to show that "ace in the hole" that is proof against sheer physical strength, the verbal thrust that ends the argument and, he suggested, is more often the weapon of the female than the male. In the essay he introduced his sister, Lynn; his mother; and his first wife, Lindsay Crouse, as experts in the use of this verbal weapon, but he also laid claim to it himself. In fact the final paragraph of the essay places Mamet himself firmly in the category of bitchiness, as it describes being seated at a restaurant table with an attractive female stranger who maintained a truculent silence, which he took personally. As he rose to pay the check, he said, "Nice chatting with you," and she looked at him and said, "My best friend died today," his response being "Hey, Bitch, *I* didn't kill her" (49). Mamet explained the dynamic: "Laugh if you will, cry if you must, but I like to think, like bitches everywhere, that my quick and elegant rejoinder raised that woman from the morass of her legitimate personal problems, and enmired her in mine" (49).

That Mamet placed his sister, his mother and himself among those who make use of this no-holds-barred verbal assault as a superior weapon to physical abuse is no accident. In *The Cabin* his most revealing, and most often anthologized, essay, "The Rake," describes a family dynamic in his and Lynn's childhood with their mother and stepfather that was replete with physical and emotional abuse. "The Rake" focuses on three incidents that resonate profoundly, suggesting a family environment that did tremendous damage to both children, but to Lynn especially. They depict a physically violent and emotionally out-of-control stepfather and an emotionally remote mother who was resentful and jealous of her children. Both parents would seem to have been happy if the children had disappeared, which Mamet in fact did, going to live with his father at the age of fourteen; he felt very guilty later in life for having abandoned his younger sister. In the episode to which the title refers, the children were told to rake the lawn, and David, angry over something, threw the rake at Lynn, who had her lip badly cut by a piece of its metal binding. Because their mother refused to take Lynn to the hospital until they told her what happened and, fearing the punishment David would face, neither of the children would say, they were forced to sit through dinner as Lynn held a napkin to her face while the blood soaked through and dripped into her food. They went to the hospital only after the dinner was finished and the plates were cleared. Lynn at another time was thrown against the wall by her mercurial stepfather. She broke a vertebra in her neck but was forced to walk to school the next day anyway, her pain considered the punishment for her transgression, which was to point out too triumphantly that she could not have committed some misdeed of which he had accused her.

Mamet described the dinner table as the locus of most of their trauma. His stepfather often smashed the table's glass top out of rage at the children, which they were given to understand was their fault. In one incident their mother called the high school and told the drama teacher that Lynn could not perform the lead in the school play's opening night because she could not eat all of the dinner her mother had prepared. The symbolism of this traditional site of family bonding and maternal nurturing becoming the site of physical trauma, emotional abandonment, and parental jealously resonates powerfully in the essay. It is reflected chillingly in the "family joke" that was played when they went out to dinner, the parents in the car, pulling away just as the children were about to get into the back seat, over and over again.

The incident that most powerfully shows the sickness at the core of this family, however, is an emotionally traumatic scene that was witnessed by Lynn as a small child. Getting up in the middle of the night and looking for comfort, she opened the door to her parents' bedroom to find her mother lying in a fetal position on the floor of the closet and sobbing uncontrollably as her stepfather stood over her elderly grandfather, sitting on the bed, while he kept repeating that he could not say the words "I love you" to his daughter. For witnessing this scene, the stepfather hit Lynn with a hairbrush and pushed her out of the room. Later in the essay, Mamet explained that his grandfather had engaged in the same ritual weekly beatings of his mother, the "naughty child" (8), that his stepfather administered to Lynn on Sunday nights after he had taken his own children back to their mother. The essay ends with a powerful image of the childhoods destroyed behind the domestic facade of the "model home" in the Chicago suburbs. What Mamet remembered was walking home from school along what was then a cornfield on the edge of the prairie in the viciously cold Chicago winters: "From the remove of years, I can see how the area might and may have been beautiful. One could have walked in the stubble of the cornfields, or hunted birds, or enjoyed any of a number of pleasures naturally occurring" (11). For these two children, such pleasures were not unthinkable—they were just never thought of.[5]

The Theater

Mamet has written a number of personal essays about the theater and its artists, for whom he has always expressed great respect and affection. He has written, "my closest friends, my intimate companions, have always been actors. My beloved wife [Rebecca Pidgeon] is an actor. My extended family consists of the actors I have grown up, worked, lived, and aged with. I have been, for many years, part of various theatre companies, any one of which in its healthy state more nearly resembles a perfect community than any other group that I have encountered."[6] Over the years he has written nostalgically about his early days in the theater, as a student at New York's Neighborhood Playhouse, as a factotum in the Cherry Lane Theater, and as one of the founders of a small theater company in Chicago. He has written appreciatively about such theatrical heroes as Tennessee Williams and Anton Chekhov, whose plays he has adapted, as well as long-time collaborators such as director Gregory Mosher and actor William H. Macy.

Mamet's writing about the theater has evolved, however, along with his views of theater, film, and television, and he does not trouble himself about consistency with his earlier opinions when his views change. A good example of this is his attitude toward the influential teacher and theorist of acting, Constantin Stanislavsky, and the Method, an American acting technique that was inspired by his ideas. At the Neighborhood Playhouse during his college years, Mamet studied under Sanford Meisner, one of the most respected teachers of the Method. His early essays on acting express respect for both Stanislavsky and Meisner, but in the early 1990s he changed his mind about the Method, with its introspective, emotional approach to acting, and rejected it in favor of a simpler, more direct technique. In *True and False: Heresy and Common Sense for the Actor*, he wrote categorically that "'emotional memory,' 'sense memory,' and the tenets of the Method back to and including Stanislavsky's trilogy are a lot of hogwash. This 'method' does not work; it cannot be practiced" (12). Instead of trying to recapture his own emotional experiences to display on stage, he wrote, "the actor is onstage to communicate the play to the audience. That is the beginning and the end of his and her job. To do so the actor needs a strong voice, superb diction, a supple, well-proportioned body, and a rudimentary understanding of the play" (9). Instead of trying to "become" the character, he said, the actor needs to recognize that "there *is* no character. There are only lines upon a page" (9). This is a tenet he has repeated many times, in reference to film as well as theater. Its corollary is that detailed research into the play and the attempt to create backstory for the characters in order to understand their actions and emotions is a waste of time. From Mamet's point of view, once the actor has learned the lines, the important things all take place on stage between the actors or, more important, between actor and audience.

To go with his views on acting, Mamet has articulated a similarly straightforward description of the drama. In *Three Uses of the Knife: On the Nature and Purpose of Drama,* he has argued against a social or didactic purpose for the theater, asserting that "the purpose of art is not to change but to delight. I don't think its purpose is to enlighten us. I don't think it's to change us. I don't think it's to teach us" (26). He also has stated that "the purpose of theater, like magic, like religion—those three harness mates—is to inspire cleansing awe" (69). His model is the community ritual of tragedy. Like Aristotle, whom he admires, he places a great emphasis on dramatic structure, which he finds organic to human experience and perception. He wrote that "dramatic structure is not an arbitrary—or even a conscious—invention. It is an organic codification of the human mechanism for ordering information. Event, elaboration, denouement; thesis, antithesis, synthesis; boy meets girl, boy loses girl, boy gets girl; act one, two, three" (73). Although he has some interesting things to say about the nature and purpose of the second act, the play's middle and traditionally the most difficult for the playwright to write, he emphasizes that it is the ending of the play that is most important. What we have created in the drama is "the opportunity to face our nature, to face our deeds, to face our lies [. . .] for the subject of drama is The Lie." At the end of the drama, "THE TRUTH—which has been overlooked, disregarded, scorned, and denied—prevails. And that is how we know the Drama is done. It is done when the hidden is revealed and we are made whole, for we *remember*" (79).

Religion, Identity, and Politics

Mamet has been writing about his Jewish identity since the 1980s. In *Some Freaks* he described his parents, second-generation Americans who were "in the rabid pursuit, first, of education, and then, of success, greatly assimilationist" (8). It was a generation that was "largely Reform; and thought themselves 'racially' but not 'religiously' Jewish" (8). To Mamet this meant that "among ourselves, we shared the wonderful, the warm, and the comforting codes, language, jokes, and attitudes which make up the consolations of strangers in a strange land," such as "Jewish humor, a pride in each other's accomplishments, a sense of sometimes intellectual and sometimes moral superiority to the populace-at-large" (8–9). At one further remove, for his generation, he wrote, "Jewish culture consisted of Jewish food and Jewish jokes, neither of which, probably, were very good for us" (9). He complained that the Jews in the Reform temple of his youth seemed to be ashamed of being Jewish. The rabbis were addressed as "doctor," and the children went to Sunday school rather than shul. On the whole, "Judaism, at my temple in the 1950s, was seen as American Good Citizenship (of which creed we could be proud), with some Unfortunate Asiatic Overtones, which we were not going to be so craven as to *deny* [. . .] we would go by the name of Jews, although every other aspect of our religious life was Unitarian" (17). In short, he said, he found the Reform Judaism of his childhood "nothing other than a desire to 'pass'" (17).

Mamet has voiced similar feelings over the years, particularly disappointment in Jews who fail to embrace their Jewish identity and institutions, such as the Jewish-dominated movie business, which conspire to suppress the Jewish identity of their participants. On the other hand, he admires "those in all generations who have embraced their Jewishness. We are a beautiful people and a good people, and a magnificent and ancient history of thought and action lives in our literature and *lives in our blood*" (13). In *South of the Northeast Kingdom,* he mentioned with great warmth the friends and neighbors whom he identified as part of a Jewish community around the village of Cabot, Vermont. The culmination of Mamet's writing about these issues so far has come, however, in *The Wicked Son,* the title of which refers to the ritual question of the second son at the Passover feast, who asks, "What does this ritual mean to *you?*" and thus "removes himself from his tradition, and sets up as a rationalist and judge of those who would study, learn, and belong."[7] He addressed the book to the wicked sons among American Jews:

> To the Jews who, in the sixties, envied the Black Power Movement; who, in the nineties, envied the Palestinians; who weep at *Exodus* but jeer at the Israel Defense Forces; who nod when Tevye praises tradition but fidget through the seder; who might take their curiosity to a dogfight, to a bordello or an opium den but find ludicrous the notion of a visit to the synagogue; whose favorite Jew is Anne Frank and whose second-favorite does not exist; who are humble in their desire to learn about Kwanzaa and proud of their ignorance of Tu Bi'Shvat; who dread endogamy more than incest; who bow the head reverently at a baptism and have never attended a bris—to you, who find your religion and race repulsive, your ignorance of your history a satisfaction, here is a book from your brother. (xi–xii)

Mamet stated a proposition for the wicked son: "The world hates the Jews. In or out" (7). The book consists of thirty-seven short pieces that are aimed at bringing the *apikoros,* or fallen away Jew, to see the error of his or her ways and return to the fold. He offers it because "there are issues upon which one must take a stand. One of them, I believe, is that of Jewish identity; for not to do so is to remove oneself from the group" (138). And belonging to the group is for Mamet a central part of the religious experience. As he wrote, "the Jew is not only made and instructed but also *commanded* to live in the world and to enjoy those things God has permitted him—among the chiefest joys: that of belonging" (169).

Although the ideas expressed in *The Wicked Son* came as no surprise to those who knew Mamet's work, the book was received with bemusement by many reviewers, particularly those who wrote for Jewish periodicals and websites. Several reviewers commented that they had not known Mamet was Jewish, one noting that "the author comes off quite perceptibly as a Ba'al Teshuvah [a Jew who has returned]. I see it in his eagerness to educate, his invigorating dedication to Torah, his fire (attributes which benefit his arguments), but I also perceive it in his naiveté, his simplified understanding of biblical commentary and scholarship, and his still evolving and maturing religious outlook."[8] Less diplomatically Lawrence Bush suggested that "not since flying monkeys attacked Dorothy and her crew has a straw man been set upon with such vehemence [. . .] this most modern of playwrights and film directors writes like one of the pioneering Zionist theorists of the late 19th-century."[9] The *Toronto Star* complained that "this book boils with bile. Over its 37 short chapters Mamet manages to call non-observant Jews ignorant, obdurate, hurtful, treasonous, racist, lost, self-loathing, arrogant, shrinking, shameful, blind, confused, remorseful, hateful, pathetic, slothful, muddle-headed, afflicted, vile and a plague."[10] Referring to Mamet's presenting it as "a book from your brother," another remarked, "more like 'here is a book that your brother is hurling across the table at your ugly face!' Mamet's brotherly scorn extends way beyond his self-hating straw man to the entire liberal American Jewish landscape."[11] Several wondered about the book's efficacy in accomplishing Mamet's goal. "It's difficult to imagine Mamet will change many lapsed, anti-Zionist minds with this bellicose and venomous frontal assault on secular Judaism,"[12] wrote Joe Eskenazi in San Francisco's *Alternative Online Daily News*.

Mamet was taken to task by more than one reviewer for his lack of scholarship, what one called his "intellectual laziness and, frankly, clumsy thinking."[13] Several complained that he did not present a sustained argument in the book, but a series of "short op-ed-like chapters,"[14] although one reviewer recognized it as consciously rooted in the philosophy of *chazarah*: "teach the lesson over and over until it penetrates the layers of passivity and indifference, apathy and cynicism. Repeat the message until it is driven into the active consciousness."[15] Another complaint was that "belonging, not believing or behaving, is the only aspect of Jewish identity to which Mamet truly testifies."[16] Much of this dissatisfaction comes from mistaken expectations about what Mamet was trying to do. *The Wicked Son* is not a scholarly book. It is, like most of Mamet's prose writing, a distinctly personal book, a passionate declaration of his own dedication to Judaism and an in-your-face challenge to his formerly fellow secular Jews, "in or out." Both declaration and challenge are characteristic of Mamet's writing.

Mamet's well-established role as cultural contrarian and provocateur was further bolstered by his 2008 article in the liberal *Village Voice*, "Why I Am No Longer a Brain-Dead Liberal." In this short essay, he repudiated his former state as a blind adherent to what he took to be liberal political principles and announced that he agreed with the conservative ideas of Thomas Sowell, Milton Friedman, Paul Johnson, and Shelby Steele. He recalled a moment of epiphany that linked his growing political conservatism with his passionate feeling for his Jewish identity. Listening to NPR while driving in the car, he found himself responding with physical tension, which his wife described as "Shut the fuck up."[17] The source of Mamet's anger is summed up in his reference to NPR as "National Palestinian Radio." Mamet has identified support for the state of Israel as a central element of Jewish identity, and no one receives greater opprobrium in *The Wicked Son* than the Jewish supporter of the Palestinians. Linking support for the Palestinians with liberalism proved an entrée into a reexamination of what, "as a child of the '60s," he took to be the liberal articles of faith: "that government is corrupt, that business is exploitative, and that people are generally good at heart." Thinking it over, he found that he does not believe that people are good at heart. In fact he thinks that "people, in circumstances of stress, can behave like swine, and that this, indeed, is not only a fit subject, but the only subject of drama," a subject that has informed his own writing for the last forty years. Although he affirmed the U.S. Constitution, he also expressed his mistrust not only of the then-current administration of George W. Bush, but of all government, and he was "hard-pressed to see an instance where the intervention of the government led to much beyond sorrow." As an alternative to the government's intervention, he affirmed the power of the citizens to "work it all out," making a surprising analogy with the theater: "take away the director from the staged play and what do you get? Usually a diminution of strife, a shorter rehearsal period, and a better production." He also said that his view of the military and of corporations had changed from negative to positive, and, on the whole, "things appeared to me to be unfolding pretty well."

As might be expected, this essay was received with delight by the political Right. The *New Criterion* wrote that Mamet's essay "gives one faith in human nature. It may not, this side of paradise, be perfectible, but clearly it is educable."[18] "Welcome home, David Mamet," wrote Dinesh D'Souza.[19]

Perhaps Mamet has found, in his sixties, a political home in the twenty-first-century brand of U.S. conservatism, just as he has found a home in Judaism and Jewish culture and tradition. One theme that runs consistently through Mamet's prose is the desire for a home, the need to belong. Whether writing of the pleasure of feeling at home among a group of men engaged in some manly activity or of his love for the different communities to which he confidently belongs—a theater or film company, a synagogue, his own family—this need to belong is ever-present in his personal essays, as is his seemingly constant search for a new group with which to feel at home. It would be too easy to ascribe this psychic need to the early loss of his childhood home, but that loss is certainly a factor. There is great pleasure in his descriptions of these groups and communities, but there is also a great hunger to be accepted and loved. Mamet might have found a home among the conservatives in 2008, but, given his capacity for changing his mind as he confronts new experiences, ideas, and facts, it is not likely to be his last.

CHAPTER 3

Men with Men, Women with Women

David Mamet is well known for the all-male-cast plays that he has written throughout his career. These include *Lakeboat* (1970), *The Duck Variations* (1972), *American Buffalo* (1975), *A Life in the Theatre* (1977), *Prairie du Chien* (1979), *Glengarry Glen Ross* (1983), and *The Disappearance of the Jews* (1997), as well as several more short plays. Mamet has clearly been interested in the world of men, creating, from the beginning of his career, a "homosocial order," which David Radavich has analyzed.[1] Mamet has characterized two of his earliest plays, *Lakeboat* and *Duck Variations,* as naturalistic slices of life meant to emphasize character.

Lakeboat 1970

Lakeboat was the second full-length play Mamet wrote. The first was *Camel,* a review influenced by the work of the improv troupe Second City, where he had worked during his high school years in Chicago. At Goddard College, where he majored in English, Mamet talked his professor into allowing him to write a play for his senior thesis, and *Camel* was the result. *Lakeboat* was written after his graduation from Goddard, when he wrote to some friends at nearby Marlboro College to see if he could be hired as an actor for their summer theater. As Mamet explained to Mark Zweigler: "They said no, but the fellow who ran the drama department was leaving on sabbatical, and he asked me if I would like to teach. I said I'd love to. He wrote back asking if I had anything specific to recommend me, and I said I had just written a new play. I hadn't, but he said that was great and that I could come to Marlboro and produce it. In the interim I worked on a bunch of notes concerning my stint in the Merchant Marine and made them into a second play, called

Lakeboat."[2] *Lakeboat* was first produced in 1970, while Mamet was teaching at Marlboro.

Based on Mamet's then-recent experience of working on an ore boat on the Great Lakes, *Lakeboat* is an intensely personal play. He later described it as one of his "feeling slices of interesting life [. . .] episodic glimpses of humanity."[3] The play is a series of twenty-eight brief scenes, some less than a page of dialogue, dramatizing the interactions of the sailors on the lakeboat *T. Harrison*, "the floating home of 45 men" (135).[4] The play is often perceived by critics as unstructured. Of the quite successful 1998 production in London, for example, Sheridan Morley wrote that "there's no real plot here, just eight men in conversations and monologues trying to make some kind of sense out of their lost opportunities, friendships, and in some cases lives."[5]

As Christopher Bigsby noted in his perceptive analysis of the play, however, *Lakeboat*'s episodic form embodies a deep and meaningful structure that may not be apparent at first viewing: "The very structure of *Lakeboat* implies a discontinuity which becomes a basic characteristic of the figures [Mamet] creates, a fragmentation which is presented as social fact (a sense of alienation bred out of American myths of competitive capitalism), psychological reality (men and women divorced equally from one another and their own sexuality) and historical truth (they are cut off from a sense of the past)."[6] Beneath the fragmentation Bigsby has found a principle of coherence in the dialogic technique of storytelling. For Bigsby storytelling is a fundamental element in the construction of Mamet's dramatic world, evident from the beginning in this, his first major play. For his characters, "story becomes a substitute for what is so manifestly absent from their own lives—a sense of coherence, meaning and communication. It also fills a silence which otherwise carries its own threat."[7]

Beneath the episodic structure of *Lakeboat*, there is indeed the clear arc of a story, and this deep dramatic structure is based on storytelling itself. The story of what has happened to Guigliani (or Guilini, Guliami, or Guiglialli), the boat's night cook who has failed to turn up as it is about to embark on a voyage from East Chicago, Indiana, to Duluth, Minnesota, is the narrative element that connects the scenes. The Guigliani tale links the play's first and last scenes and forms the substance of various narrative performances throughout the play by the Pierman, the Fireman, the second mate Collins, and Fred, one of the sailors. Beginning with the Pierman's rendition in the first scene, which Mamet entitles "What Do You Do with a Drunken Sailor?," the story of Guigliani takes on the characteristics of folklore as it undergoes a series of transformations during the recitations by several people who do not really know what happened. The Pierman creates a gory tale in which Guigliani gets drunk in a bar and is robbed by a prostitute. Beaten and bloodied, he is delayed from boarding the ship by the guards at the gate and is finally thrown in the canal by order of the first mate. This is shown not be true when Skippy, the first mate, asks where he is. The second mate tells him he got mugged and is in the hospital.

Fred, who has deep worries over gambling debts, tells a version in which Guigliani is beaten to a pulp by the Mafia. The fireman, who spends his four-hour shifts staring at four gauges in the engine room or reading to relieve the boredom, dreams up a mysterious tale in which Guigliani had a gun that he brought to a bar, but he did not have it when they found him, attributing his disappearance to "the cops" or "Uncle Sam" because "he knew things" (197) and was probably on the run. In the final scene, as Dale, the young man who is replacing Guigliani, discusses his death with Fred, Joe, another sailor, arrives with the anticlimactic news that they will be picking him up in Duluth because he took the train there after he missed the boat. Joe says, "Skippy said he said his aunt died, but he thinks the *real* reason 'cause he overslept" (211).

Michael Hinden has suggested that the Guigliani story "reflects the crew's communal endeavor to construct a myth that has the effect of glamorizing their shared fate. In the end, the tale remains an empty one, but it illustrates the potential of the crew to cohere through the shared medium of language"[8] (41). This is an optimistic view of the crew's interactions. The shared myth that they create ("What You Do with a Drunken Sailor") expresses less a shared community than a collective imagination that conceives of life as predatory, violent and dangerous. The men see themselves at the mercy of exploitation and assault from the people they encounter on shore and inexplicable dismissal by the authority figures of the shipping line.

Two additional narrative threads that give coherence to the play's episodes suggest this view as well. Joe Litko, the older sailor who confides in the newcomer, Dale, and tries to take him under his wing, is revealed, despite the surface banality of the dialogue, to be a deeply unhappy man. The alcoholic son of an alcoholic father, he was working on the boats when he was in his teens; he reveals to Dale that his fondest dream had been to be a ballet dancer. He tells Dale about his previous thoughts of suicide and asks him about the availability of morphine on the ship. He also talks to Collins about the possibility of drowning. Fred, the sailor in his thirties who fears the Mafia, reveals that he has just lost seven hundred dollars at the racetrack, and he says he pays eighty dollars per month in child support, a large sum for a sailor in the 1970s. He tells Dale about a sailor who was paid thirty-six hundred dollars in compensation for two fingers he lost in a winch. Sensing that Fred sees this as a way out of his troubles, Dale tells him, "I wouldn't do it at all. Even by accident. No amount of money [. . .] You can't buy a finger, man. It's gone and that's it. Not for all the money in the world" (203).

In addition to the narrative coherence achieved through the gradually revealed stories of the men, Mamet uses the autobiographical character Dale as an element of focus and continuity. As a middle-class student who works on the boat as a summer job between the first and second years of college, Dale has more in common with the typical theater audience than with the sailors. In the 1981 reading version of the play, Mamet emphasized Dale's outsider status by beginning the play on his first day and having him address the audience directly as a narrator in the mode of Tennessee Williams's Tom Wingfield. In revising the play for the 1983 acting version of the script, Mamet cut the first scene, making for a more direct engagement between the audience and the sailors.

It is important to note that in *Lakeboat* Mamet has not written a naturalistic exposé of the hopeless lives of working sailors. He presents these men with too much depth, vitality, and humor for that. And he makes clear that even the depressive Joe has moments of transcendence in his life. Talking about the Mackinac Bridge, he remarks to Dale, "we been going under that bridge for once or twice a week since I was your age off and on, but that sure is a pretty bridge [. . .] this beauty of it makes what it does all the more . . . nice" (190). After decades on a boat hauling ore around the Great Lakes, Joe has not lost the aesthetic sense of the would-be ballet dancer.

For a second play, and one written clearly from a young man's point of view, *Lakeboat* is a remarkably mature work. Several critics have noted that it has many of the characteristics that would become the signature elements of Mamet's dramaturgy. The use of episodic structure is something Mamet would continue to develop throughout the 1980s and 1990s. As Johan Callens has suggested, *Lakeboat* "anticipates many of the concerns that would reappear in his work, dealing, as it does, with an all-male world in which language and power are intimately connected, a world in which story telling plays a central role for characters vaguely aware of the insufficiency of their lives."[9] The homosocial world of male camaraderie that masks the missing intimacy and sense of loss noted by Bigsby and the sense of failed community delineated by Hinden is explored in much of Mamet's later work.

Also present here are characteristics that would provoke a good deal of controversy throughout Mamet's career. Charges of misogyny were made against this play in which women enter the conversation of the men only as drunken, thieving whores, exploitative ex-wives, drunken or ineffectual mothers, girl friends who need to be treated "like shit" (162), or, most notoriously, "soft things with a hole in the middle" (166). Alain Piette has pointed out that the language of the play, in which, as Fred says, the men "say 'fuck' in direct proportion to how bored they are" (160), was shocking to audiences in the 1970s. Largely because Mamet has elevated the use of obscenity to an art form, audiences have become so accustomed to it that it now goes unnoticed in his plays. As Piette has noted, "Mamet's obscenities contribute to a sense of verisimilitude but they are also at the heart of a quasi-hypnotic rhythm. The actors whom Mamet has directed in his productions of his own work have spoken of his beating out the rhythm of the obscenities."[10] In the relationship between Dale and some of the older sailors, particularly Joe, there is also the student-teacher dynamic that Mamet would explore overtly in *Squirrels, A Life in the Theater,* and *Oleanna,* as well as in relationships such as that between Don and Bobby in *American Buffalo* and Levene and Roma in *Glengarry Glen Ross.*[11]

What is arresting in this early play is the development of a dramaturgy that accommodates not only the combination of these disparate influences but Mamet's direct experience as well. Despite the careful construction of the dialogue to produce rhythm and evoke emotion and laughter from the audience—and this is one of the funniest of Mamet's plays—each of the twenty-eight scenes comes across as speech, direct and immediate. Every moment of the play feels real. It is this uncanny ability to create a believable reality through dialogue that is perhaps Mamet's greatest gift as a dramatist. And it was clearly evident from the beginning.

The Duck Variations, 1972

Mamet told Charlie Rose that he wrote the first version of *Duck Variations* in Vermont "about 1968 or 1969,"[12] and it was first produced at Goddard College when he was teaching there in 1972. He also said that he had worked on it in Chicago, however, and he has told of typing out the scenes on the typewriter in his father's law office at odd times. The inspiration for the play was listening to old Jewish men, particularly his grandfather, talk when he was young. Its setting, "a Park on the edge of a Big City on a Lake,"[13] is probably Chicago's Lincoln Park, which Mamet knew well from his high school days at Francis Parker School, which borders the park, and later living in the Lincoln Hotel, which looked out on the park, its zoo, and Lake Michigan "for various years of [his] youth," where he found the living arrangement "a paradise."[14] When he lived at the Lincoln, Mamet "wrote sitting on various benches in the park,"[15] where he could have seen many friends like his two characters Emil Varec and George S. Aronovitz, "two gentlemen in their sixties" (73), sitting together companionably. A major structural influence on the play, with its fourteen "variations" in place of scenes, is the music theory and composition that Mamet studied in his youth. "My writing is influenced by musical ideas, resolutions, phrasing," he said in an early interview.[16] Several strong literary influences on this early play, particularly those of Beckett, Pinter, and Albee, have also been noted by critics.[17]

The Duck Variations has elements that would have been characterized as absurdist in the 1970s, particularly the action of whiling away the time in conversation while "nothing happens" and the use of conversation to evade the elephant in the room for these two aging men, the illness and death they see in their future. The action of the play is simply fourteen conversations between the two, during which they talk about ducks, among other things. There is a trajectory to the conversations in which George keeps forcing the reluctant Emil to face the inevitability of the duck's death and, by implication, his own. But the two friends talk about more than death. One of the most important exchanges, a duet where they contribute equally, rather than the typical "variation" that is dominated by one man with the other responding, is about friendship. The two men are in such uncharacteristic agreement that they finish each others' sentences:

EMIL: [. . .] It's good to have a friend
GEORGE: It's good to be a friend.
EMIL: It's good to have a friend to talk to.
GEORGE: It's good to talk to a friend.
EMIL: To complain to a friend . . .
GEORGE: It's good to listen . . .
EMIL: Is good.
GEORGE: To a friend. (97–98)

The only other conversation in which the two men are so in sync is the narrative about hunters killing a duck that George tells from the point of view of the hunter: "You lift the gun, you put the gun on your shoulder and point it at the duck. It's you and him. You and the duck on the marsh. He wants to go home and you want to kill him for it. So you fire the gun" (121). Emil keeps asking "Where's the duck?" until George is forced to say, "The duck is dying":

EMIL: Out in the marsh.
GEORGE: Out in the marsh.
EMIL: Oh no.
GEORGE: In a flock of feathers and blood. Full of bullets. Quiet, so as not to make a sound. Dying.

EMIL: Living his last.
GEORGE: Dying.
EMIL: Leaving the Earth and sky.
GEORGE: Dying.
EMIL: Lying on the ground.
GEORGE: Dying.
EMIOL: Fluttering.
GEORGE: Dying.
EMIL: Sobbing.
GEORGE: Dying.
EMIL: Quietly bleeding.
GEORGE: Thinking.
EMIL: Dying.
GEORGE: Dying, dying. (121–22)

In the course of this exchange, Emil brings George around from the point of view of the hunter, to whom the duck is just a pile of feathers and duck shot out in the marsh, to that of the duck, who goes through the process of dying, anthropomorphically "sobbing." It is George who ascribes "thinking" to the duck, allowing Emil for the first time to acknowledge that he is dying. Emil tries to alter the narrative, suggesting, "But wait! This here! He summons his strength for one last time" (122), and a couple of other narrative gambits, but George keeps responding "No," until Emil finally admits, "He's dead, isn't he?" (123). George simply nods, and Emil responds "I knew it," while George observes, "The Law of Life" (123), which is the title of a well-known story by Jack London about a moose that dies valiantly under the assault of a pack of wolves.

This anthropomorphizing suggests, of course, that Emil and George are projecting their anxieties about their own lives and fear of death onto the birds they talk about, distancing themselves from memories and fears about the future. Specific dangers to the ducks that they decry are equally threatening to them as human beings. George brings up the pollution from all the "gook" in the stratosphere, and he tells a tall tale about ducks with lung cancer who looked at hunters "like they were trying to bum a smoke" (92). Emil speaks of the polluted lake and oil slicks that produce "oil-bearing ducks floating up dead on the beaches. Beaches closing. No place to swim. The surface of the sea is solid dying wildlife" (106), but then he turns around and complains that no one can burn leaves in the fall anymore. At one point he tells George that he is upset by his talk "of nature and the duck and death. Morbid useless talk" (96).

Although their meditations end in an acknowledgment of death, it is the whole cycle of life represented in the duck that interests the two friends. The play takes place around Easter, a mythic time for the affirmation of the life cycle, and in the first variation George comments that the ducks are "a sure sign of spring," but Emil reminds him, "Autumn too" (79). They talk about the migration of the ducks, about the leader who "learns the route. Maybe he's got a little more on the ball" (80) than the other ducks, replacing the leader who has come before him, and in turn being replaced:

GEORGE: He dies, he leaves . . . / something. And another duck moves on up.
EMIL: And *someday.*
GEORGE: Yes.
EMIL: Someone will take *his* place.
GEORGE: Until . . .
EMIL: It's boring just to think about it. (81)

As counterpoint to the orderly cycle of the duck's life, the predictable patterns of migration and the orderly cycles of the generations, the second variation evokes its Darwinian struggle with the blue heron, a favorite bird image of Mamet's, which George insists is the "hereditary Enemy of the Duck" (82). The battle between the two, he says, "is as old as time. The ducks propagating, the Herons eating them. The Herons multiplying and losing numbers to exhaustion in the never-ending chase of the duck. Each keeping the other in check, down through history, until a bond of unspoken friendship and respect unites them, even in the embrace of death" (83). When Emil asks why they continue to fight, George responds, "Survival of the fittest. The never-ending struggle between heredity and environment. The urge to combat. Old as the oceans. Instilled in us all. Who can say to what purpose?" (83).

This conversation leads to Emil's observation in the third variation that "Every blessed thing [. . .] that lives has got a purpose" (85), concluding with the assertion that "the law of the universe is a law unto itself [. . .] And woe be to the man who fools around" (87). Although Emil and George express things in their own colorful idiom, the moral of their musings is very close to that of London's story, an affirmation of "the law of life," which includes the "boring" nature of the biological and generational cycles, the struggle for survival, and the inevitability of death. Within this paradigm, however, Emil and George make a space for human feeling. Just as they invest the duck's death with human emotion, they insist that the heron and the duck, predator and prey, must be united by "an unspoken friendship and respect" (83).

The final variation, which follows the death of the duck, is about the ancient Greeks, "Old. Old men. / Incapable of working. / Of no use to their society" (124) who, Emil says, used to watch the birds all day, "First Light: Go watch birds. / Last light: Stop watching birds. Go Home" (125). He says the Greeks would "sit on a bench and feed them," just as George and Emil do. He describes the birds and the old men watching each other, "Each with something to contribute. / That the world might turn another day" (125), which Emil says, is a fitting end "To some very noble creatures of the sky. / And a lotta Greeks" (125). Although death has been acknowledged, it is an affirmation of the daily cycle of life to which Emil comes in the end. As boring as it is, he comes to believe, their daily routine is after all worthwhile. It is certainly as crucial to the Law of Life as death is.

Coming twenty-five years after *The Duck Variations, The Disappearance of the Jews,* the first of the three plays that make up *The Old Neighborhood,* is a another two-hander, a conversation between Mamet's recurring autobiographical character, Bobby Gould, and the old friend of his boyhood and youth, Joey Lewis. While he is going through a divorce, Bobby has returned to Chicago to renew his ties with old friends and family. This play takes place in a hotel room and consists of a single conversation between Bobby and Joey. They reminisce about their boyhood and about various girlfriends they had as young men, but the conversation keeps returning to the question of their Jewish identity and what it means for them. From their talk about who is Jewish and who is "goyish" in the movies and their reminiscences—centering on beating up Howie Greenberg at camp, going to Temple Zion, the Jewish identity of the man who owned the shoe store, and dating two folk dancers, Debbie Rosen and Debbie Rubovitz, whom they cannot tell apart—it is clear that they share a past that was decidedly Jewish, but they are confused about its meaning for them and their current connection to the Jewish faith and traditions. Bobby has married a "shiksa," who once suggested to him that, since the Jews have been persecuted for so long, they must have brought it on themselves. Now that he is divorcing her, he is concerned about his son's identity. While he insists that "the kid is a Jew," Joey reminds him that "the law says, he's a Jew his mother is a Jew."[18] Bobby responds, "fuck the law" (14) and cannot imagine that any child of his would not be Jewish: "They start knocking heads in the schoolyard looking for Jews, you fuckin' think they aren't going to take my kid" (14).

Both of the men are fundamentally unhappy, admitting to occasional suicidal thoughts. Joey dreams of living a life with a "connection [. . .] where their lives are a joy. Where questions are answered with ritual. Where life is short" (33). He wishes he could have been born in Europe in the old days, living a simple life in the shtetl. He thinks he would be a great man in the village, working on a forge all day, and the people would say, "There goes Reb

Lewis, he's the strongest man in Lodz" (19). Bobby wishes he could have been in the movie business in the 1920s, saying, "Jesus, I know they had a good time there. Here you got, I mean, five smart Jew boys from Russia, this whole industry" (25). Both men are looking for some meaningful connection to their faith to stave off their existential angst. Joey fantasizes about leaving his wife and family and tramping off into the Canadian wilds with a pistol with which "I can end it any time. I feel so free" (31). He knows that there are holy men and visionaries who are that free, but he also knows that he is "going to die like this. A shmuck" (31). He and his wife have just joined a synagogue, a gesture toward some kind of connection, but they have not prayed there yet. Bobby says that he invents ceremonies for prayer, but he can never remember to keep them up. Significantly the two make a date to visit Waldheim, the cemetery where Joey's father is buried, as a sort of ritual that honors a faith that both seem to know is dead. Like Emil and George, however, Bobby and Joey share something that Mamet suggests is important. They are friends. The past lives in their reminiscences and their stories about it. Their shared experience is a Jewish experience, despite the fact that they may have "disappeared," as Jews, into a homogenous, agnostic, American life. Bobby's son is, after all, a Jew, despite what the law says.

Boston Marriage, 1999

When *Boston Marriage* was first produced, in Boston in 1999, and especially when it was produced in New York in 2002, many critics saw it as Mamet's counter to the perception that he is unable to create fully developed female characters and the charges of misogyny that had dogged him since the seventies, coming to a head with *Oleanna* in 1992. As Jeremy McCarter wrote, "detractors have long said Mr. Mamet can't write roles for women; he has responded with a play about two feuding lesbians and their maid [. . .] it has enough ebullience to make up for its shortcomings. All parties seem to have— if you'll permit me—a gay old time."[19] Once again, however, Mamet's treatment of women engendered controversy. Several critics expressed the view that if *Boston Marriage* was written to combat the notion that Mamet is a misogynistic writer, it has had the opposite effect. Michael Feingold wrote that "the piece seems alternately like a tribute to women and a sneering gibe at them."[20]

Boston Marriage is written in the comedy of manners style. As the reviewers noted from the beginning, its style and humor owe a great deal to Oscar Wilde's epigrammatic and paradoxical dialogue. The opening scene between Anna and Claire, former partners in a Boston marriage, the nineteenth-century term for two women who live together in an intense friendship that may or may not have a sexual dimension,[21] provides a number of Wildean exchanges such as this repartee about the enormous emerald necklace Anna has been given by her "Protector":

CLAIRE: Might I be forgiven to ask: Is it Real?
ANNA: My dear, I have not lost my Taste . . .
CLAIRE: Then you have lost your virtue . . . ?
ANNA: Yes.
CLAIRE: Thank God.
ANNA: A man gave it to me.
CLAIRE: A man.
ANNA: They do have such hopes for the mercantile.
CLAIRE: And those hopes so rarely disappointed.[22]

Like one of Wilde's comedies, its plot is so contrived and improbable as to parody the traditional comedy of manners. It opens with Claire's arrival and with Anna's good news about having secured her Protector, who has cleared her debts, given her an account at the dressmaker's, and settled a monthly income on her as well as presenting her with the enormous emerald, which he has told her is a family heirloom. Anna suggests to Claire that the two of them could live comfortably on her newfound income. Claire has news of her own, however. She is in love, and with a girl so young she is still chaperoned by her mother. Claire has come to ask Anna to let her use her house to meet the girl. Anna is devastated by this news and by the idea that "You Want me to Be Your Beard [. . .] you wish me to clothe your nakedness" (27). She reminds Claire that such a thing would "*endanger* my, my compact with my New Protector," an arrangement she entered only "for us, for that unity-of-two" (28). Eventually she agrees to participate in the scheme, saying "this is the new thing, then. This is that for which it has amused God to spare me [. . .] I shall grant graciously what I dare not refuse" (32).

The plot takes a turn at the end of act 1, with Claire's startling curtain line after the girl's arrival, "She asks why you are wearing her mother's necklace" (42). In act 2 Anna and Claire try to find some way of controlling the damage from their exposure. With a nod to Mamet's *The Shawl*, Anna comes up with the improbable scheme of pretending to be clairvoyant and telling the girl her father brought the emerald to them so they could divine her mother's "secret ills, and their alleviation" (75). Then she says Claire should pretend to be a fortune-teller so they can explain the girl's presence to the father by telling him she came to consult Claire.

This scheme is aborted when a letter from her Protector's attorney arrives, and she learns that the entire family has "decamped," and he has "terminated the, the 'consultation fees,' which, of late, it has been his use to pay" (92), and he requires the immediate return of his wife's necklace. Anna is forced to recognize that she was "mistaken in his steadfastness" (93). Claire urges her to keep the necklace, declaiming: "Are all our possessions, and all our joys, but loaned on *sufferance,* and subject to the whim of men? He's broke his promise. He's deceived you. He's had the use of your body, and he paid for it with stolen goods. For God's sake keep the necklace" (94). But, with a newfound moral sense, Anna insists that she cannot because "it was not his to give" (93). Anna seems to have a moment of enlightenment when she suggests that "*true* happiness might lie . . . not in obtaining the, the object of one's" lust, but "in being *free* of it. Would *that* not be joy?" Claire responds, "No" (95), but Anna persists, and she goes to get the necklace.

Another turn of the plot comes when Anna returns, saying that she has been robbed of the necklace and she will go to prison. When she finds that Catherine, the maid, is missing, Claire assumes she has taken the necklace and gone off. Expressing her admiration that Anna has forgiven her for wronging her, Claire says that she will accompany Anna to prison. When Anna leaves to get her wrap, Catherine appears, ready to make tea, and tells Claire the necklace is in the Bible, where Anna was using it as a bookmark. When Anna returns, Claire does not tell her she knows about the necklace but says she will be honored to accompany her "into Exile" (112) and will never leave her. The two embrace and go out to sit in the park, but Anna and Catherine reenter, and Anna tells her that someone will come for the jewel, which is still in the Bible. The play ends with an ongoing sexual joke, as Catherine tells Anna, "your friend's forgot her muff," and Anna then replies, "that remains to be seen" (113).

The play's parodic spirit was noted from the beginning, with reviewers referring not only to Wilde, but to Henry James and, in Charles Isherwood's case, to writers as varied as Ronald Firbank, Ivy Compton-Burnett, Joe Orton, Charles Ludlam, and "various Victorian melodramatists."[23] Maurice Charney has suggested that *Boston Marriage* is "overtly a parody of Restoration comedy of manners as filtered through Oscar Wilde's enormously influential *Importance of Being Earnest* (1895)."[24] Though this is certainly true, looking at the play through this lens does not fully account for the depth of its parodic nature or the complicated aesthetics of Mamet's dramaturgy. In parodying Wilde, Mamet recognizes Wilde's own parodic spirit. *Earnest* is, after all, "a trivial comedy for serious people." It parodies the conventions of comedy of manners, but it takes deeper aim at Victorian society, suggesting that the marriage provided at the end as one of the conventions of comedy is a trap in which the free spirit will be smothered in convention. In one sense the moral of Wilde's play is that if a man is going to marry, he had better be acquainted with "bunburying"—that is, he had better have some avenue of escape, the implication being to a free-wheeling homosexual subculture.[25] Wilde's evocation of the gay male subculture of Victorian England has its counterpart in the lesbian subculture evoked in *Boston Marriage*. The women are, as Claire says, "a small band of Freebooters" (38). What Anna wants, however, and what Claire finally agrees to, is *marriage*, a committed relationship. The way they get there is partly through the wildly improbable comic plot, but also, and more interestingly, through a more deeply embedded parody of classical tragedy.

Mamet introduces the tragic with Claire's suggestion at the beginning of the play that Anna is "tempting fate" with her overconfidence in her arrangement with her Protector. "He worships me. What could go awry?," says Anna, and Claire introduces the element that will actually be their undoing: "Has he, for example, a wife?" (6). At the beginning of act 2, when she has just been exposed, Anna gives a speech that parodies the protagonist's moment of anagnorisis, or revelation, in classical Greek tragedy: "Oh, fate inexorable. Oh, fate misthought at first to be but circumstance, revealed at last as the minute operations of the gods. Oh fate but our own character congealed into a burning glass. Focus your cleansing light upon me, and I shall be cleansed" (51). When Claire complains that Anna is denigrating her loss of the daughter by her "display of equanimity in the face of your own [loss]" (56), Anna replies that she has experienced a "reversal" (56), the second of Aristotle's requirements for a tragic plot. After the letter arrives, dashing their hopes of salvaging the daughter, the Protector, or the emerald, Anna tells Claire that they could "intuit, in this Reversal, the, the operations of a Greater Hand [. . .] A Brake, or Governor, upon . . . Both our, I believe it. Happiness and Folly" (101). Like a Sophoclean hero, she imagines herself living out her days peacefully in an Inn, where she could be happy "as long as one has not 'done evil' [. . .] caused *pain*" (98).

Anna compares herself to Ulysses. She must "bind [herself] to the mast" (13) to listen to Claire's tale of falling in love. Claire, on the other hand, is associated with Prometheus. Before she knows about Claire's new love interest, Anna says that her return is like that of Prometheus, "Who brought fire to the gods" (7). Claire reminds her that he stole fire *from* the gods, and this is what Mamet's imagery suggests about her. Claire notes that Anna goes cold at the announcement that she is in love. With Claire's arrival the stove has gone cold, as has the tea. Because Anna has turned her anger at Claire toward Catherine, she fails to warm up the tea, and Anna observes that the tea will remain cold, blaming herself "and an impersonal, and thoughtless deity" (30).

When Anna proposes a little party featuring a pie, Claire counters with ices, suggesting that what Anna finds abhorrent about them is their frigidity. If the cold is associated with Anna's loss of Claire, Claire's passion for the Protector's daughter is figured by the flame of a candle. When Anna recognizes that Claire must really love the girl, she offers her the comfort of having her "In Retrospect [. . .] as, do you see, as the vision of a flame. Which persists. After the flame is gone [. . .] the *vision* of the flame" (100–101). This is not enough for Claire, who has partly been attracted to the girl because of her own fear of aging. She says that she has lost her, "and with her, the last good instant of my youth" (96), later lamenting, "Oh, Age, Age, Dreadful Age" (98). She is, she says, "a plague upon the rocks" (100), again suggesting the fate of Prometheus.

In a thematic thread that is typical of Mamet, he uses the emerald, a traditional symbol of jealous passion, also as a signifier of the reduction of human relations to commercial transactions. Anna mistakes the emerald for proof of love, insisting that her Protector's wife does not "hold his affection" because she does not wear the jewel. Claire later says that the emerald, as it signifies her Protector, is "the ensign of that selfishness, that Jealousy Engendered by Wealth" (38). It is, of course, the emerald that betrays them when the man's daughter sees it. Anna quickly decides to give up the emerald as meaningless: "What care I for the loss of a Jewel? Let him restore it, to his 'wife,' or . . . *whatever* employee of his he has filched it from" (49). Later the emerald forms a central part of the scheme to trick the Protector's daughter, as they plan to use it as a crystal ball to divine her mother's "secret ills" (75), but when Anna finds that the jig is up and the scheme is useless, she willingly gives up the jewel.

Both of the women are redeemed, in some sense, when they rise above their appetites and self-interest. Claire finally confesses to Anna, "I am the cause of your misfortune. If I had not brought the child here, does not such a speech occur to you?" (106). Anna's response is not to attack, but to forgive her: "None of us is perfect. Each is not only permitted but required to repent . . . And if to repent, then of necessity to err. It is now my lot to attempt that most profoundly difficult of human tasks" (106). Claire responds, "To forgive one who has wronged you?," and Anna responds with a Wildean "No, to pack when rushed. What shall I want in a cell [. . .] I'll take your portrait" (106), signifying that Claire is forgiven. For her part Claire offers to accompany Anna to jail, not knowing at this point that, because the jewel is safe, there is no danger of jail. At the end of the play, she is given one more chance at youth, when a message comes that the girl is waiting for her and will continue to wait for just one minute. She tells Catherine that there is no answer, making it clear that she has given up the girl for Anna.

There is a Mametean turn on this redemptive renunciation, of course, because each of the women is also pulling a con job on the other. Anna has known all along that the jewel is safe, and she is playing on Claire's sympathy to get her to come back. At the end of the play, Claire withholds the information that Catherine has told her where the jewel is, saying that she would be "not resigned, but honored" to accompany Anna into exile (112). On the other hand, a balance is reached when Claire says that she cannot promise that her feelings will never change, but she says that she will never leave, and Anna says, "I am content" (113). The play thus fulfills the plot conventions of both comedy and tragedy. The couple, Anna and Claire, overcome the potential blocks to their happy union, the commodification of sexual desire represented by the Protector and his emerald and the blind lust for lost youth represented by his daughter, to form an enduring marriage. Anna has also gone through a reversal of fortune that has given her a greater understanding of life and a new sense of moral values and has resulted in a peaceful resignation to the limitations of fate. That both resolutions have been achieved through deception suggests Mamet's corrective insertion of his perception of the way the world works into these traditional forms. Claire's pragmatic worldview will be a corrective of Anna's idealism: "The world you see is not cruel. It possess neither falsity nor guile. And it shall be my mission to protect you from it" (112).

The subplot of Anna and Claire's interaction with Catherine provides another locus for these issues. At the beginning of the play, it seems that Catherine is there to function as a signifier of class, a reminder of the callous disregard that these well-off women have for their servants. When Anna is angry with Claire, she abuses Catherine, calling her "Bridey" and "Mary" and "Nora" and delivering diatribes about the Irish, completely ignoring Catherine's insistence that her name is Catherine and that she is Scottish, not Irish. The satirical humor here is directed at Anna's complete insensitivity toward the humanity of her servant. At the end of act 1, following her rejection by Claire, Anna cooly propositions Catherine in exchange for "a secure position"(42), and Catherine promises to think about it, a purely mercenary exchange that mirrors Anna's relationship with her Protector. When Catherine tells her that she has been "ruined," Anna fires her and hypocritically tells her, "go, go, go, go away, you sad, immoral harlot" (67), but this edict is withdrawn when she finds out Catherine can help with the deception in the séance.

Mamet takes the relationship beyond the satirical when it is Catherine who articulates the vision that leads to the redemption of Claire and Anna. She repeats a saying of her Auld Gran: "Life is Froth and Life is Bubble. Two things stand like stone. Kindness in another's trouble. Courage in your own" (69). This maxim leads Claire to the realization that they have fallen victim to "the worst sin" (69), that of despair, and that they must help themselves. If it is a form of kindness, the ability to think beyond self-interest, that allows Anna to forgive Claire in the end, it is courage that enables Claire to decide to accompany her to jail. Without these two acts of virtue, the happy ending could not occur. And Catherine is rewarded as well. As she makes plans to meet her "feller," Claire asks her, "What in life is not a compromise?," and Catherine replies, "Love." Claire responds with uncharacteristic human feeling and a newfound sincerity, "May you find it so" (111).

Art: *Squirrels,* 1974; *A Life in the Theatre,* 1977

Squirrels takes place in a writer's office, where "*an old writer*" Arthur is collaborating with "*a young writer*" Edmond.[26] With many narrative variations, Arthur constantly repeats the same sequence of events, in which a man sits on a park bench, watching the squirrels. He clucks to draw a squirrel to him, and as he moves to stroke the squirrel, it bites his hand, and then he grabs the squirrel and squeezes it until it dies. The core story becomes the vehicle for a number of aesthetic disagreements between the collaborators, the main one being that Edmond constantly wants to know the meaning or moral of the story, and Arthur insists that there need not be a meaning or a moral, because "One writes what one feels" (9) and "art is art" (23). The Cleaningwoman, a writer herself who claims to have been Arthur's lover at some point, tells Edmond that Arthur "is dead and dried and hung in the freezer of forgotten dreams" and advises Edmond to "hit the fuckin' highway quicker than it takes to tell" (25).

Later Arthur admits that his creative powers are diminishing, confessing to the Cleaningwoman that he may be losing his "ability to generalize" (41). When she tells him, "you still got your old way with an adjective," he responds, "there's more to life than a facility with modifiers. It's possible that I've lost the touch. (*Pause*) Once broken, never mended" (41). As this play was written during the heyday of structuralist theory and when Mamet was involved with academia, it is no surprise that Arthur is preoccupied with form and formalism. His treatment of the core squirrel story is like the reduction of a narrative to a series of tropes as performed by a member of the Prague School, which of course empties the narrative of the "meaning" that Edmond is always looking to supply. In a parody of such operations on the text, early in the play, Arthur suggests that "for the purpose of simplicity [. . .] we can divide these four figures into two distinctive units [. . .] one unit can consist of two men [. . .] the second unit shall consist of the remaining man and the squirrel" (11). When Edmond threatens to leave Arthur because he is not happy writing the same story about squirrels all the time, Arthur insists that he is not fixated on squirrels, and that if it is the squirrels Edmond objects to, they can move on to another animal: "Can you truly feel that I'm limited? When you've been in the business as long as I you will not feel that way" (45). To keep Edmond from leaving, Arthur pretends to be able to write about something else, and he dictates a passage the Cleaningwoman has left in the wastebasket. In their final scene, they are writing about geese, but it is Edmond who is doing the writing. In his one attempt at a creative contribution, Arthur has the character say, "I almost saw a squirrel today that looked like a small dog" (49), a theft from the Cleaningwoman, who had said the same thing about a horse (47). Even here he is unable to write about anything but squirrels.

A Life in the Theatre depicts the relationship between an older actor, Robert, and a young actor, John, during a season of performances in a repertory theater. Its twenty-six scenes were originally set in a variety of locations, but Mamet got the idea from Gregory Mosher, the play's original director, to set all of them in a theater. Some of the scenes re-create the performances of the actors in the less than stellar plays the repertory company is performing; some show the actors rehearsing on the empty stage; most are set in their shared dressing room, where their relationship progresses throughout the season. Robert tries to play the role of mentor to John, calling on the privilege of his seniority and his greater experience in the theater to give advice and make sententious speeches about the theater and the art of acting. Much of Mamet's dialogue is seemingly banal and superficial, the daily interchange of two actors who share a dressing room and strike up a casual friendship that includes going out for meals after the show. Beneath the superficiality there is a good deal more going on, of course. The struggle for dominance that is characteristic of Mamet's male characters emerges, as does the sense that, beneath the avuncular confidence he displays toward John, Robert is in a depressed and increasingly desperate state of mind. During a performance he loses track of where he is in the play, insisting on repeating a scene they have already done. He cuts his wrist with a razor in what is an apparent attempt at suicide, but he denies it and keeps repeating to John that he is tired. Robert is clearly troubled and probably a deeply depressed man, and he is on the verge of losing his memory and thus the one thing that sustains him, his career in the theater. The play ends with his summing up of his life—"Ephemeris, ephemeris. (*Pause.*) 'An actor's life for me.'"[27]

In both plays the focus is on the interaction between the two characters, attempts by the older artists to remain "in the game" by demonstrating their superior knowledge and creative power to the younger artists, attempts that ironically reveal the decline of their artistry and serve as the vehicle for the ascendancy of the younger men to dominance in the relationship and the rejection of their claims to mentorship. Both plays focus on the effect that the artist's human relationships have on his diminishing capacity as an artist.

Both *Squirrels* and *A Life in the Theatre* present what purports to be a mentorship relationship, in which the older artist tries to teach the younger one, passing on the knowledge gained from a lifetime of practicing his art. Both plays, however, reveal a cruel displacement of the older artist as the younger artist finally rebels against his assumption of authority and rejects the lessons he is trying to impart. In *Squirrels*, Edmond begins as a kind of apprentice to Arthur, taking his dictation, making neutral sounds such as "Mmmmmm," and asking an occasional question. Arthur encourages him by telling him he is "doing quite well" (10), and Edmond apologizes when he interrupts with an idea. As he becomes increasingly tired of the squirrel scenario, however, Edmond tries to intervene in the narrative, first asking if he can "try one" and then becoming increasingly insistent on his interventions, trying to bring human emotions and motivations into the story. Arthur ignores him and finally exerts control by ending the session and pulling the schoolboy bully trick of making Edmond give him his lunch to eat. In their second session, it is Edmond who is offering a narrative about a man and woman meeting in the park, but Arthur insistently brings it back to the squirrel narrative. When Arthur asks Edmond, "Have you learned nothing working here?," Edmond says, "No" (33).

When Edmond finally tells Arthur he is unhappy because he is "sick of the squirrels" (46) and Arthur is "very overbearing" (45), Arthur gives in and, in order to keep Edmond with him, reads him the Cleaningwoman's fragment about moonlight on the ocean that he finds in the wastebasket, implying it is his. In the following scene with the Cleaningwoman, Edmond is quite happy as he tells her they are writing about geese, calling it "forward motion" (47). Edmond, however, begins to take on Arthur's aesthetic stance, questioning his own earlier insistence on meaning and saying that artistic development is difficult to perceive and that perhaps perception is not crucial to the artist. In a string of theoretical gibberish and clichéd phrases about art, he arrives at the notion that "a period of . . . work . . . untempered by harassing elements of . . . introspective examination can be beneficial [. . .] that is, it is potentially not the least valuable aspect of this hiatic (non-introspective) period that it becomes, eventually, instructive. To the creator" (47–48). He ends with a position that is identical with Arthur's, but, because he is a young man of his generation, it is obfuscated with confused "theoretical" thinking. He says that

"because I did the work and didn't worry those elements once only philo-
sophic and ideal about which I wasted so much thoughts [sic] have become
osmosed into my being as technique and are behind me" (48). He declares
that there is strength in technique, and, echoing Arthur, that "the true employ-
ment of inspiration is in formal endeavors where the inspiration can take
form" (48).

To prove to the Cleaningwoman that they have been working, Edmond
quotes a poetic passage, saying "I wrote that" (48). But the passage is actually a collaboration involving Edmond, Arthur, and the Cleaningwoman. It is
cut down from the lines that Arthur plagiarized from the Cleaningwoman's
discarded fragment, with the addition of a line about geese. In the final scene
between Edmond and Arthur, the two have completely reversed roles, as
Edmond goes on about "Geese Geese Geese. Close in formation. Promoting
order" (48), and Arthur, after his futile attempt to start a new story with a reference to squirrels, is told to type up the lines about the geese. In a sense
Arthur's mentorship has succeeded: he has turned Edmond into the same kind
of writer he is. But in the process Edmond has assumed ascendency in their
relationship. It is he who makes the claim to creativity; it is he who assumes
an overbearing attitude toward Arthur, and Arthur is reduced to mere amanu-
ensis. The passage they end up with is ridiculously banal: "Geese geese geese.
Flying over park and lake. Over sand and water. Over sea and shore, young
and old, lion and tiger. Searching searching searching. Seaching to be free"
(49). Nevertheless the scene ends with a long pause in which they *look at
each other with satisfaction"* (49). The symbiosis has achieved a balance. In
shaping his "Johnnie-Come-Lately" pupil into the formalist writer he would
like to be, Arthur has achieved the goal of his mentorship, an aesthetic dominance over the next generation. By asserting his control over the subject matter and inserting "meaning" into the composition through the motive of
"searching to be free," Edmond has achieved dominance in the relationship
with Arthur, the young man taking power away from the older one.

Interestingly it is the Cleaningwoman who has the last word. Throughout
the play her narratives show the most imagination and vitality. They range
from a story about sex to a Western to the romantic passage that Arthur pla-
giarizes to a Civil War story and then an adventure story involving the Royal
Canadian Mounted Police. All these things are bad, but they have great
energy and imagination, two things that Arthur and Edmond clearly lack. The
play ends with the Cleaningwoman's squirrel poem:

> Squirrels. (Squirrels.)
> Gatherers of nuts.

Harbingers of autumn.
Clucking and strangling.
Strangling and being strangled.
Rushing to your logical conclusion.
Searching to be free. (50)

What the Cleaningwoman does is endow a meaning to the squirrel story that Arthur has insisted is meaningless. In "Rushing to your logical conclusion / Searching to be free," the Cleaningwoman articulates two of the fundamental human preoccupations that are articulated in literature: the teleological awareness of fate or inevitable death that informs the tragic and the naturalistic, and the vital desire for freedom from constraint and the dominance of the older generation that informs comedy. Of course the line "searching to be free" is one that comes from Edmond's lines about the geese. Whether this is collaboration, intertextuality, signifying, or simple plagiarism, the point is made that all these writers depend on each other's work in order to write their own. In the end the Cleaningwoman tosses this poem into the wastebasket before she nods to the audience. After seeing a performance of the play, Mamet added the line, "or words to that effect,"[28] after the poem, emphasizing the arbitrariness of the language and the contingency of the work of art.

In his introduction to *A Life in the Theatre*, Mamet wrote that advice that he heard from Sanford Meisner while he was a student at the Neighborhood Playhouse was his inspiration for the play:

"When you go into the professional world, at a stock theater somewhere, backstage, you will meet an older actor—someone who has been around awhile.

"He will tell you tales and anecdotes about life in the theater.

"He will speak to you about your performance and the performances of others, and he will generalize to you, based on his experience and his intuitions, about the laws of the stage. Ignore this man." (105)

Of course, in assuming the role of mentor on the strength of his experience in the theater, Meisner was doing exactly what he was telling his students to ignore, and Mamet, his student, was not ignoring it. Mamet also wrote of his time as a very young man working in the off-Broadway theater, when older actors in the company performing *The Fantasticks* "were more than nice to my incredibly green self"[29] (Mamet, *Make-Believe Town* 33). The ambiguity in these statements is reflected in the relationship between Robert and John. Robert is clearly a lonely man, who in his mature years is far from the pinnacle of success in his career. In John he befriends a young actor who benefits from his knowledge, but he also fulfills his own emotional need to feel that he is influencing, as he puts it, "young people in the theatre . . . tomorrow's leaders" (6). Robert gives John tips about fencing, coaches him through a movement workout, and tries to offer literary insights about the plays they are rehearsing. His most intense teaching, however, is reserved for John's instruction about the acting profession. "We must support each other, John. This is the wondrous thing *about* the theatre, this potential" (24). He insists on etiquette in the dressing room, declaring, "one generation sows the seeds. It instructs the preceding . . . that is to say, the *following* generation . . . from the quality of its actions" (56). He insists that "there must be law, there must be a reason, there must be tradition" (57) in the theater and in society at large.

John is at first grateful for the attention from the older actor. His attitude toward Robert is respectful, attentive, even tender. He praises Robert's work and is shyly pleased to be asked out for a meal. He lights Robert's cigarette, cleans some stray make-up from his face, and in a scene that David Radavich calls "the most penetrating stage metaphor of homosexual interconnection in all of Mamet's work,"[30] even pins the broken zipper of his fly in the midst of escalating double entendres, ending with Robert's line, "Oh, fuck you. Will you stick it in?" (34). The tension in the relationship begins to emerge in scene 6 as Robert shows some jealousy of a "friend" with whom John makes a date, and in scene 8, as John rebels somewhat against Robert's dominance of the dressing room and his suggestion that John "do less" in a scene they have together. This rebellion ends in the zipper-pinning incident, however, reestablishing Robert's dominance, as he stands on a chair while John performs this service.

In scene 17 John, finally fed up with Robert's pronouncements about the theater, responds to a voluble meditation on greasepaint with the words, "Would you please shut up?" (55), prompting Robert's lessons on etiquette, to which John responds guardedly. In scene 22, Robert's professional unease erupts, as he remarks that John has been praised too much in the reviews. The scene ends with a rupture as Robert calls John a "fucking TWIT" (70) and John tells him not to use his towels anymore. This scene is followed by the turning point in their relationship, when John, who has landed a better acting job, is rehearsing *Henry V* while Robert eavesdrops. Mamet has written of this turning point as "the moment of the recognition of mortality, at which moment the younger generation recognizes and accepts its responsibilities, and the older generation begins to retire."[31]

Throughout the play John has been rather guarded, speaking little and responding with monosyllables or clipped neutral phrases to most of what Robert says. Peter Evans, who played John in the first New York production in 1978, said that John's attitude toward Robert is ambiguous. "John is very *careful;* he wants to learn as much as he can. We talked about my respect for Robert, a senior member of the company, one whose approval I needed."[32] In this scene Robert lays a claim on John, reminding him that what happens on stage is part of his life, "which is one reason I'm so *gratified* (if I may presume, and I recognize that it may be a presumption) to see you . . . to see the *young* of the Theatre . . . (And it's *not* unlike one's children) . . . following in the foot-paths of . . . following in the footsteps of . . .those who have gone before" (72). John responds to this naked plea for recognition and affection by merely saying goodnight, and then Robert breaks down in tears when John catches him watching him rehearse from another part of the theater. Like an insecure lover, Robert pleads, "You're not angry with me, are you?" (74), and later, when it is clear that he still has not left the theater, John says "(*sotto voce*) Shit" (75). In the following scene, when Robert forgets where he is in the play and keeps insisting on John's cue for an earlier scene, John whispers, "We've done that one, Robert" (78), and when Robert keeps insisting, John simply walks off the stage.

John's engagement with the older actor ends with its usefulness. The sym-biosis of the mentor relationship, with the green young actor's seeking the tips about the profession that the older man can give him and the older actor's seeking a disciple to keep his work alive in the theater, is no longer balanced. Robert's human needs have become too pressing, his instruction more annoy-ing than helpful. Now that he is losing his competence as an actor, Robert is an encumbrance holding back John's career. In the final scene Mamet makes it clear that the roles have been reversed. In the first scene John is not eating well because he is nervous. In the last scene, it is Robert who is not eating. John is going out after the show, not with him but with "some people" (84). Robert has become the subservient one, lighting John's cigarette and lending him money for his evening out. It is not that John is cruel, but he has the cal-lousness of youth and the ego of the artist, now confident in his talent. He is intent on his career, and Robert serves no further purpose for him. In the final scene Robert's plight is pathetic, his treasured "life in the theatre" a romantic notion that covers the reality of a cutthroat business that "eats the orange and throws the peel away," as Willy Loman says, like any other. The play implies that the valued commodities in the theater are talent and youth. Robert never had much of the first, and he has lost the second. It is John's turn now, and he will never be Robert's child.

CHAPTER 4

Men and Women

Mamet has written so effectively about the world of men and of male relationships that it has often been said he is not interested in writing about
women and that he is not capable of creating a fully developed female character. Given his reputation as the prototypically male playwright, it is interesting to consider that, particularly at the beginning of his career, Mamet
wrote intensively about the relationships between men and women. The character Ruth in *The Woods* may be unique among Mamet's early plays for its
definition and depth, but that character has since been matched by characters
such as *The Cryptogram*'s Donny, *Oleanna*'s Carol, the two women in *Boston
Marriage*, *The Old Neighborhood*'s Jolly and Deeny, and various film roles.

Among Mamet's plays from the 1970s, *Sexual Perversity in Chicago* and
The Woods are the most focused and sustained efforts to dramatize the relations between men and women, but early Mamet one-acts such as *The Sanctity of Marriage* and *Prairie du Chien* cast some chilling light on heterosexual
relationships within marriage. *All Men Are Whores,* in a series of vignettes
that suggest the darker side of the humorous *Sexual Perversity,* exposes the
occasions for heartbreak and exploitation amid the play's myriad examples of
sexually driven behavior, passion, selfishness, vulnerability, and rejection. The
vignettes range from sadomasochism and other violent sexual fantasies to
casual sex that leaves the participants yearning for a fuller connection, to callous breakups, to the memories of a series of romantic nights on the beach. It
ends with the female character musing, "what if this undignified and headlong
thrusting toward each other's sex is nothing but an oversight or physical mal-
formity? (*Pause.*) Should we not, perhaps, retrain ourselves to revel in the sexual act not as the consummation of predestined and regenerate desire, but
rather as a two-part affirmation of our need for solace in extremis [. . .] in

which we render extreme unction with our genitalia."[1] As ham-fisted as that metaphor is, it suggests something of Mamet's quest in all of these plays. Discussing *The Woods* in an early interview, he said it was a play about heterosexuality, "which is just not a hot theatrical topic over here [in the United States]. It is something that you look at in the popular media, a subject that people would rather not address—why men and women have a difficult time trying to get along with each other."[2] It was a subject that was intensely interesting to him in the 1970s.

Sexual Perversity in Chicago, 1974

Mamet's first entry into the field of men and women was, at least in tone, a comedy. In thirty-four scenes *Sexual Perversity* dramatizes the interrelationships among four young Chicagoans in the early 1970s: Dan Shapiro, "an urban male in his late twenties"[3] who is an assistant office manager; his friend and coworker Bernie Litko, a few years older; Deborah Solomon, an illustrator; and Joan Webber, a kindergarten teacher. Some of the play's scenes are several minutes long; others are single monologues or brief exchanges between two characters. The structure owes a good deal to Mamet's experience with the fast-paced scenes and blackouts of the improv troupe Second City, where he worked busing tables while in high school. Most of the scenes are funny. Anne Dean has noted the connection between the play's structure and its theme: structured in swift, short scenes that rise, like dirty jokes, to punchlines, the play examines the void at the heart of contemporary sexual relationships. Life for Mamet's characters is as shallow as the fictional lives of their soap opera heroes and incorporates many aspects of an obscene joke; their exploits are crude, debased, and usually over very quickly. The form and shape of the play are themselves reminiscent of such jokes, and so the very structure of the piece enacts its meaning.[4]

In the course of the play, Danny breaks away from Bernie, his clueless mentor in all things sexual, and opts out of the singles-bar scene, with its anonymous hook-ups, to try to form a more meaningful relationship with Deborah. Joan, Deborah's roommate, tries to talk her out of moving in with Dan, and then she predicts that the relationship will last two months. She proves prescient as, after the first sensual glow wears off, Deb and Danny are unable to communicate with each other in any meaningful way, and their relationship deteriorates. After the couple parts, Joan tells Deborah, "in the end, what do you have? You have your friends" (60), and the play ends with Danny and Bernie ogling women on a beach.

Mamet has said that the play is "just, unfortunately, tales from my life [. . .] My sex life was ruined by the popular media. It took a lot of getting over.

There are a lot of people in my situation. The myths around us, destroying our lives, such a great capacity to destroy our lives."[5] In discussing the theme of the play, Mamet has emphasized the importance of language: "Voltaire said words were invented to hide feelings. That's what the play is about, how what we say influences what we think. The words that the older [character] Bernie Litko says to Danny influences [sic] his behavior, you know, that women are broads, that they're there to exploit. And the words that Joan says to her friend Deborah: men are problematical creatures which are necessary to have a relationship with because that's what society says, but it never really works outs [sic]. It's nothing but a schlep, a misery constantly."[6]

This summary seems a strange description for a comedy. Christopher Bigsby has suggested that the play is in fact deeply ironic: "much of the play's humour derives from the characters' failure to understand themselves or other people, the ironic space between a confident language of sexual aggression and a fumbling incompetence when confronted with the reality of potential relationships."[7] His comment is true, but, in a dynamic that is similar to the one Eric Bentley has described for farce, the surface humor of the language proceeds in turn from the deep anxieties of the characters about sexuality, human relationships, and their own identities, anxieties that Mamet ascribes to the social pressures and myths with which his generation was raised: "James Bond fucked up my sex life for years," he complained.[8] Mamet acknowledged that what pervade the play are "the myths that men 'go through.' [. . .] You have to sleep with every woman that you see, have a new car every two years—sheer utter nonsense. Men never have to deal with it, are never really forced to deal with it, deal with it by getting colitis, anxiety attacks and by killing themselves."[9]

Mamet describes the characters as if they were a modern versions of Renaissance humour characters: "Joan intellectualizes everything, Debbie uses catch phrases, Danny jokes things away, and Bernie tries to overpower everyone."[10] Critics have in fact compared the play to both the comedy of Ben Jonson and the homiletic tragedy of the Renaissance, a descendant of the medieval morality play.[11] David Skeele contends that Bernie's main action throughout the play is to corrupt Danny, "tearing him away from his one chance at salvation" through a "genuine connection" with Deborah. For him, "Bernie *is* Sexual Perversity."[12] From Skeele's point of view, the play is a tragedy, with Bernie the primary agent of Danny's fall and the two characters ending up in a particularly appropriate hell at the end: "sitting in blazing heat, surrounded by beautiful women that they will never be able to touch."[13] A great deal of Skeele's reading rings true, but there is still the fact that the language is deployed in the service of humor rather than tragic seriousness. Bert

Cardullo suggested a reading of the last scene that is not tragic so much as per-haps a deeply ironic, "perverse" comedy. He described the structure as a twist on the old Hollywood formula, boy meets girl, boy loses girl, boy gets girl. In this case, "Bernie has Danny, loses Danny (to Deborah), regains Danny, and Joan has Deborah, loses Deborah (to Danny), and regains Deborah"[14]

Cardullo resisted the idea that the same-gender relationships in the play have a sexual dimension, but sexuality has been a controversial question since the play was first produced. In early reviews Michael Feingold suggested that "Bernard has latent homosexual tendencies,"[15] and Edith Oliver went further, assuming that "the subtly pointed incidents are so unobtrusively put together that for quite a while the audience is unaware that [. . .] these couples are homosexual."[16] More recently David Radavich has suggested that Mamet's characters are more accurately understood using Eve Kosofsky Sedgewick's definition of a homosocial bond, in which two men negotiate their relation-ship to each other through the medium of a sexual relationship with a woman. Radavich suggests that in *Sexual Perversity* this triangulated forma-tion works itself out in a context in which "a desire for dominance, usually between men of unequal rank or age, battles with an equally strong desire for loyalty and acceptance, resulting in a hard-won, intense, fundamentally unsta-ble intimacy established in the absence of women."[17]

The question remains, are the characters homosexual, "latent" homosex-ual, homosocial, or uncomplicatedly heterosexual? Mamet's play, which is extremely overt about heterosexual sex, does not suggest any sexual activity between same-gender couples, but he did insert a few teasers to hint at the possibility of same-sex desire. As a gambit for fending off Danny's initial advances in the library, Deborah claims to be a lesbian. Later, in bed, she tells Danny, "I'm not really a Lesbian [. . .] But I have had some Lesbianic experi-ences [. . .] and I enjoyed them" (26). In the postcoital context, it is impossi-ble to tell which, if any, of the three statements is true. Joan has been identified as a lesbian by critics more often than Deborah has because of Joan's dissat-isfaction with men and the intensity of her complaints about them, as well as her clear disturbance and overt jealousy when Deborah moves in with Dan. Both of the men show some hints of homoerotic desire. Dan rather shyly questions Bernie about whether he "fooled around" with other boys when he was young, and Bernie, who has no trouble supplying graphic details about his supposed encounters with women, tries to convey the nuances of his activ-ity through the implications of the words "fooling," "messing," and "fuck-ing" around (43). Bernie is overtly homophobic, calling a gay salesperson "a fucking fruit" and "a fairy" and being upset that this man works in the toy department (42). His account of having been molested in a movie theater as a child reveals that he still bears emotional scars that come out partly in his hatred for all homosexuals. Bernie has some gleam of insight that his sexual problems may be related to this incident—"You don't learn right when you're young, those cocksuckers ruin your life" (44). When Danny suggests that "it could possibly have been damaging to you [. . .] as a total Human Being" (45), however, Bernie refuses to face this possibility: "A kid laughs these things off. You forget, you go on living . . . what the fuck, huh?" (45).

The fact is that no one in the play is confident enough of his or her sexuality to embrace an identity that deviates from heterosexuality. Characters might acknowledge a little youthful experimentation but not that a "perverted" desire is part of their make-up. Part of Mamet's subject is the inability of the characters to resist the labels, myths, prejudices, and expectations meted out by what he calls "the media," the culture in which they grew up. The characters are uneasy, unhappy, and unable to form honest, meaningful relationships—or even to communicate intimately—with others when sex is involved because they are troubled that their own experiences and feelings do not match up with the cultural myths they have internalized. So they flee to stereotypical behavior as the only available means of defining their sexual identity.

Bernie is the most obvious example of this, and the most troubled character in the play. The counterpart of his homophobia is his hatred of women. The sexual fantasies that he relates to a credulous Danny as if they were true would come across as alarmingly violent if the tone of their delivery were more serious and Mamet had not punctuated Bernie's rendition with Danny's ingenuous questions and comments. In the famous extended fantasy that makes up the first scene, Bernie tells Danny about his supposed experience of picking up a woman whom he variously describes as eighteen or twenty-five years old—simultaneously a young girl and a sexual vampire "who knew all the pro moves" (18).

Bernie's story mimics an outright battle with the woman. He portrays himself as the passive recipient of her aggressive advances, all the while not knowing whether she was "pro, semi-pro, Betty Coed from College, regular young broad" (12), which seems to exhaust the categories he has for women. After she emits "a squeal of pleasure and relief that would fucking kill a horse" (15) when he flicks her with a towel, he follows up by heaving the clock radio at her, which produces a long welt. She then puts on a World War II flak suit and insists that he yell BOOM periodically while they have sex. She calls a friend who helps out with machine-gun sound effects from the phone, and finally she sets the room on fire, and "The broad jumps back on the bed and yells 'Now, give it to me *now* for the love of Christ'" (17), which Bernie refuses to do, as he flings ten dollars at her and walks out. Danny comments blandly, "nobody does it normally anymore," while Bernie complains, "It's these young broads. They don't know what the fuck they want" (17), an odd commentary on someone who seemed to know exactly what she wanted. Expressive of his own confusion, Bernie manages to portray himself as both the victim and the victor in this encounter, drawn in by a sexual predator who knows all the pro moves, and yet refusing her the satisfaction of the orgasm she begs him for, of course depriving himself as well.

Although not as developed in a narrative sense, Bernie's subsequent stories are no less arresting and no less violent and degrading toward women. He tells of a woman who demanded that he wrap her in a bicycle chain and lock her to the radiator during sex. He tells a story about King Farouk's running a locomotive through a woman's bedroom and then whacking her on the forehead with a ball-peen hammer during sex. He talks about watching a woman with a dog, and then he is disgusted when he sees this in a pornographic movie. Taken together, Bernie's fantasies suggest an angry and violent individual, a man who hates both women and gay men and who perhaps has the makings of a serial killer. In his more immediate dealings with women, his rage and hatred are not far from the surface. Rejected by Joan in a singles bar with perhaps the most honest line in the play, "I do not find you sexually attractive" (20), Bernie unleashes his rage at her: "So just who the fuck do you think you are, God's gift to Women? I mean where do you fucking get off with this shit. You don't want to get come on to, go enroll in a convent. You think I don't have better things to do? I don't have better ways to spend my off hours than to listen to some nowhere cunt try out cute bits on me? I mean why don't you just clean your fucking act up, Missy. You're living in a city in 1976" (20–21). Bernie finishes up by calling Joan a cockteaser, and so unsure is she of her own identity and rights within the world of the singles bar that she wilts, sitting down and saying "I . . . I'm . . . I'm sorry if I was being rude to you"(21), whereupon Bernie takes his check and leaves. This rant is followed by Bernie's advice to Danny: "The Way to Get Laid is to Treat 'Em Like Shit" (22).

Mamet has suggested that it is not the overt violence and aggression of Bernie's language that is most hurtful to women. "There's a lot of vicious language in the play [. . .] The real vicious language is the insidious thing, calling somebody a little girl or this girl. That's a lot more insidious than calling somebody a vicious whore—which is also insidious, but you can deal with it."[18] Bernie's belittling of Deborah to Danny, his suggestions that their dates must be trips to the zoo or shopping, and his comment that her profession, commercial art, is "a hell of a field for a girl" (29) are all examples of his belittling women. Perhaps the most revealing language is in the final scene on the beach, when Bernie points out to Danny the difference between a "knock-out looking broad" and a "pig" (68). The first has "nice legs [. . .] very acceptable old ass [. . .] flat belly, beautiful pair of tits" (67). The second is a woman whose "legs are for shit, her stomach is dumpy, her tits don't say anything for her, and her muscle tone is not good" (68). This, he says, "makes all the difference in the world" (68), and that seems to sum up Bernie's full experience of women. Admiring a woman's breasts, he says, "with tits like that, who needs . . . anything" (69). But the ending of the play belies this assurance. As a beautiful woman walks by, the two men say hello, and she ignores them:

BERNIE: She's probably deaf.
DANNY: She did *look* deaf, didn't she.
BERNIE: Yeah. (*Pause*)
DANNY: Deaf *bitch*. (69)

It has not occurred to Bernie that the ear was a part of a woman's anatomy that he might crave, but of course listening is a form of attention from women that the two men desire and have no idea how to get.

The play's last line also indicates that Danny has come over to the dark side after his tentative attempt to form a loving relationship with Deborah. Bernie's constant undermining of Deborah has been abetted by Danny's fear of intimacy. As their relationship begins to deteriorate, he tells Deborah, "Everything's fine. Sex, talk, life, everything. Until you want to get 'closer,' to get 'better.' Do you know what the fuck you want? Push. You push me. Why can't you just see it for what it is?" (56–57). She responds with a speech that exposes the impossibility of their going any further as a couple: "I'm a hindrance. You're trying to understand women and I'm confusing you with information. 'Cunt' won't do it. 'Fuck' won't do it. No more magic. What are you *feeling*. Tell me what you're *feeling*. Jerk" (58). They have come to an impasse that neither of them is able to get over. Danny cannot tell Deborah about his feelings, and, although she feels this lack, she has no idea how to provide the emotional safety for this sort of intimacy. Their next scene together shows the two of them dividing their belongings and accusing each other of being "a lousy fuck" (59).

As Danny comes back into Bernie's orbit, Deborah comes back into Joan's. Joan is not so violent as Bernie is, but she is as alienated from men as Bernie is from women. A funny scene, where she catches two of her kindergartners playing doctor, exhibits her disgust and anger: she tries to tell them it is perfectly natural and then leads them into the other room to wash their hands, and she then calls their parents. This behavior exhibits her deep uneasiness with the human body and with sex. It is not surprising when she suggests, "it's a dirty joke, Deborah, the whole godforsaken business" (47). Her own confusion is as evident as Bernie's, but it is expressed in a more intellectualized way. She compares human sexuality to a puzzle that "has to do with an increased ability to recognize *clues* . . . and the control of energy in the form of *lust* . . . and *desire*." This, however, is a finite puzzle whose solution lies "in transcending the rules themselves . . . (*Pause.*) . . . and pounding of the fucking pieces into places where they DO NOT FIT AT ALL" (37). Perhaps the defining image for Joan is that of the old Hag in the story she reads to the children. The Hag can be beautiful during the daylight hours so that her husband and his friends can admire her or at night, but not both: "But for one half of the day I must be this old Hag you see before you" (61). This metaphor seems to be Joan's image of herself. She can act the submissive, objectivized woman when she feels she must play the part, but sooner or later, the real Joan emerges and tells what she perceives to be the truth, turning her into an ugly Hag in the eyes of the men, and even Deborah, and finally herself.

Sexual Perversity in Chicago was the first of Mamet's plays to provoke charges of misogyny against him, charges that he seemed surprised by and anxious to deny. One interviewer reported that Mamet "credited the women's liberation movement with turning 'my head around a lot.'"[19] In another interview Mamet bristled at the suggestion that the play was misogynist, insisting, "I disagree profoundly."[20] Despite Mamet's statements critics of the play have had a hard time divorcing Mamet's views from those of his male characters. Part of the reason for this is that the male characters, particularly Bernie, are so much more fully delineated than the female ones, and their language is so much more colorful and arresting. Many critics have found that the conversations between the two women do not sound authentic. In 1976 Mamet admitted that "the fleshier parts are the man parts, I'm more around men; I listen to more men being candid than women being candid. It's something I've been trying to do more of in the last few years. Women are very different from men, I think."[21] The charge of misogyny has been rather eloquently refuted by Colin Stinton, who has acted in and directed many of Mamet's plays. In an interview with Anne Dean, he said:

A lot of criticism of [Mamet's] work—especially from women—emanates from the rather incredible notion that he is somehow advocating sexist men! If anything, he is calling attention to the fact that there are sexist men and this is why they are that way, this is how their minds work. He then subjects these characters to some scrutiny [. . .] his plays always deal with the obstacles to the kind of care, kind of love and affection he wishes were there. Some people feel that because he has portrayed the world in this negative, tragic way he is somehow saying that this is how it should be. This is really ridiculous. In fact, what he does is to bemoan the fact that there is not a better world . . . he is in fact a feminist writer in that sense because he is very, very critical of males. . . . He depicts such characters to show up their fragile egos, to show them struggling to find out who they are. He tries to provide some insight into how their minds work.[22]

When he wrote *Sexual Perversity,* Mamet's quest to understand women was just beginning. He has spent most of his talent and effort as a playwright dramatizing the world of men, but as a later play such as *Boston Marriage* shows, he never lost interest in the quest.

The Woods, 1977

In some sense *The Woods* is the tragedy that is latent in *Sexual Perversity in Chicago.* Mamet has counted it among the four plays he calls classical tragedies, and he has said that he originally composed it in verse. Many of the speeches in the printed play are in fact set up as free verse. Unlike *Sexual Perversity*'s demotic rhythms, which so cannily produce a sense of verisimilitude in capturing the speech of contemporary young Chicagoans, the dialogue in *The Woods* is, like that of *The Cryptogram,* spare, minimal, cryptic, but, in a literary sense, allusive and metaphorical and in this case almost allegorical. Mamet has described *The Woods* as "a wonderful play, a very well-written play [. . .] because it has a lot of meaning. It is a dreamy play, full of the symbology of dream and the symbology of myth, which are basically the same thing."[23] Like that of *The Cryptogram,* this play's meaning is conveyed through image, metaphor, and symbolism. But although *The Cryptogram*'s meaning is metonymically tied to objects, objects that function solidly and concretely within the action of the play, the earlier play is, as Mamet says, "dreamy," and its imagery and symbolism is evoked by the characters from dreams and stories. As "a play about heterosexuality,"[24] *The Woods* takes the dilemmas of the heterosexual relationship, which the characters in *Sexual Perversity* face in the comic context of their attempts to negotiate the Chicago singles scene, and strips them of all distractions, locating the interaction between Nick and Ruth in the isolation of a cabin in the woods.

The Woods consists of three scenes, which take place at dusk, at night, and in the morning of one twenty-four-hour period. The setting is the front porch of a cabin on a lake in the woods. Nick has invited his new lover, Ruth, to stay in the cabin, which belongs to his family, for the first time. She sees this as a step toward fuller commitment in their relationship and has brought with her a bracelet inscribed "Nicholas [. . .] I will always love you. Ruth" as a surprise for him.[25] In the first scene they talk about their surroundings, particularly the birds and animals in the woods and the lake, and they tell each other fragmented stories they were told as children, she by her grandmother and he by his father. The scene ends with Ruth's asking Nick to take her into the house so they can make love, and she promises to give him her present later.

In the second scene something is clearly not well between them. Neither of them can sleep. Ruth wants to take a walk in the rain, but Nick refuses. They return again to the stories, which take a dark turn. The tension builds when Ruth tries to persuade Nick that he need not be nervous "when a thing is new" (69): "Sometimes things are different than the way you thought they'd be when you set out on them [. . .] things can be unexpected and be beautiful if we will let them. (*Pause.*) And not be frightened by them, Nick" (68). She suggests that "we all have fantasies / And dreams [. . .] I know they can be frightening. / To do them" (69). Nick responds, "you know that, eh?" (70), and then laughs at an observation she makes about the lightning, which was not intended to be funny. When Ruth gets offended and starts to set off on a walk alone, he pulls her down to the wet floor of the porch and roughly tries to engage in sex with her while she resists, and keeps repeating that they should go inside. After she disengages from him, he sulks, and she accuses him of being "mad because I wasn't wet," insisting, "you can't, just because you know, just because you *want* something . . . There is a way things are" (75). She tells him, "you can't just push me *around*," observing, "You're all inside this thing you're in. A shell, or something. You can't see. This is no good," and she tells him that his bringing her to the cabin means that he is "committed [. . .] if you are a man" (76). She gives him the bracelet, which he refuses to put on, and she tells him, "Go fuck yourself," but then says, "I love you. I love you so much. I just want to be with you. That's the only thing I want to do. I do not want to hurt you" (82). At the end of the scene, Nick tells her to leave him alone, and she decides to go back to the city in the morning.

In the third scene, the next morning, Nick tries to keep Ruth from going. He tries to seduce her, but she tells him, "you just go fuck your*self*. I'm going swimming" (102), and she confronts him with her perception of him, telling him that he is afraid of everything under his manly act and that he does not deserve her, which causes him to say she has no self-respect. She responds, "when you become bored, I am supposed to pack up and go off. / To not upset you. / I am supposed to go and drown myself. / And if I don't, I've got no self-respect" (104).

He responds, "that's right," and she swings an oar at him, saying she hopes he dies. He hits her in the mouth, knocking her off the porch into the mud. While he apologizes, she says, "I don't think you like women [. . .] You do not respect me at all" (105). After some further conversation, Nick describes to her his fantasy woman, who would ask *him* to be lovers and tell him, "I know who you are [. . .] I know what you need [. . .] I understand you" (109).

Nick repeatedly tries to get Ruth to stay, and then he tells of a dream in which the cabin is on fire and a bear comes "to crawl beneath my house. / This house is mine now. In its hole it calls me. / In the Earth [. . .] He has a huge erection. I am singed [. . .] He has these thoughts and they are trapped inside his mouth. His jaw cannot move. He has thoughts and feelings, BUT HE CANNOT SPEAK" (112). He also tells Ruth that he doesn't know what the bear wants. Hitting Nick again and again, Ruth keeps trying to get him to speak to her. He says he is insane and "going under," and then in crisis he screams, "What are we *doing* here? [. . .] What will happen to us? *We* can't know ourselves" (114). He tries to run down to the lake, but Ruth prevents him. She tells him he is just afraid, and, starting to cry, he says that he loves her, begging her to stay with him. Cradling him in her arms, she recites her grandmother's "Babes in the Woods" story, ending with the words, "The next day" (119).

Since Ruth is by far the more voluble character, the play has been seen essentially as a monologue. Linda Winer commented that, "for a while, it seemed that Mamet had written a one-character play for two people."[26] Ruth is certainly the active agent in the play, trying to get Nick to acknowledge that he is seeking love and commitment in their relationship, just as she is. It is Ruth who is the teacher, a perennial type among Mamet's characters. In the first two acts, Ruth is essentially trying to explain some things to Nick, and she does this obliquely by means of what Mamet calls the play's "symbology," the imagery of the natural world, as well as the fragmentary stories that she tells, which are made of the motifs and tropes of myths and fairy tales.

The play begins with Ruth's image of Nick's fundamental problem, his existential isolation:

> These seagulls they were up there, one of them was up there by himself.
> He didn't want the other ones.
> They came, he'd flap and get them off.
> He let this one guy stay up there a minute. (13)

This is essentially the situation between them, and Ruth is testing Nick to see if he will allow her to stay up there longer than a minute. If Nick is figured in the gull, isolated in the air, Ruth sees her own image in the fish and the water. She says she used to catch perch when she was little: "I used to clean them. I would get the smell upon my hands. When I was little. It smelled like I put my hands inside myself. I used to like to clean the fish" (28). Later she says, "I used to say that we are only fish beneath the sea. I read this book when I was small—it said that we live in an ocean made of air and we are only fish beneath the sea" (64).

Throughout the play Ruth is connected with the water, which is also connected to sexuality. When she wants to walk out to the point in the rain, a suggestion Nick resists, she describes the rain in sensual terms as "lovely. / It is poetry / The damp [. . .] we'll go out and we'll come back here and eat. / We'll have an appetite [. . .] We'll feel good" (51). Nick says that he does not want to "get wet" (50), a phrase the characters in *Sexual Perversity* use to signify casual or anonymous sex. Ruth says, "I want to be with *you* out there. / It will be wet, but we will not be *getting* wet" (51), suggesting sex as an intimate rather than a casual activity. When Nick tries to force sex on her, this sense of the water as her natural element is contrasted with the wet porch and the rain gear she is wearing, which she says is wet and sticky (72), and her insistence that Nick is mad because she "wasn't wet" (75), that she did not respond to his rough approach to sex. Water and sexuality are connected for Ruth with a sense of being part of Nature and its rhythms. When Nick comments that waves do not make a difference to the fish, "they're on the surface, but they don't affect the water underneath" (95), Ruth observes that it is only the deeper currents that affect the fish, and presumably herself.

Ruth's interest in the rain is paralleled by her fascination with the rotted rowboat she finds at the point, a boat that Nick keeps denying is theirs. Significantly the point is opposite the cove, and the two function as masculine and feminine images. After describing the boat as "real dry [. . .] very dry," Ruth says that she would like to go to sea, but "men would not let women go to sea" (16). When Nick suggests that the Vikings might have allowed this, she denies it, saying Viking women had to stay at home and make clothes, and "they used to bash the babies' heads in. / All the little girls" (17). Nick speaks of a raccoon, which gnawed its way out when trapped in a milk container, and of herons, which drag their feet when they fly—images of entrapment and of being dragged down to earth. The major natural image, however, is the bear, which figures importantly in Nick's dream in act 3. Ruth first mentions a bear, when she says that an old woman told her the cabin was built on a bear's cave, and the bear kept coming back, finally returning for the last time "to get beneath the house" to die (25). The imagery of the cave, an image of the vagina or the womb and simultaneously of the grave, and of the bear, cast in Nick's dream as the image of a threatening male sexuality, is overt. The fragile cabin built on top of the cave, a home that is in flames in Nick's dream, suggests the threat he feels to his fantasy of happiness, his dreams of "Homes and things [. . .] Living in them. Being warm" (66), with a woman he "would meet and we would just be happy" (67).

Ruth has a healthy regard for what she calls "our appetites," whether for sex or for food, suggesting that desire is "just the body's way to tell us things that we may need" (20). For Nick, on the other hand, sexual desire and the "things he wants" (112), as he says of the bear, are so threatening that he can not even speak of them. His blockage is expressed most vividly in the story he tells about his father and Herman Waltz, a war comrade who came to the cabin when Nick was a boy. Waltz believed that Hitler told him things he should do to his wife, whom he beat, and that the Martians had kidnaped him and "he had fallen from great distances. Inside their craft" (39). The story that Nick's father told him was about falling "in a hole with him," (45), one that was "Deep. Deep. Very deep" (57), where Waltz told him they would never leave alive. Nick says that it rained the whole time they were in the hole and that all Waltz talked about was his new wife, but when he got out, he beat her up, and Nick does not know why. After the war, he says, his father and Waltz "would be involved together" (37). The story is rife with sexual anxiety. The fear of falling in a hole and not being able to escape parallels the fear of death that is linked with female sexuality in the bear imagery. More interesting is the fear of loss of control, that the sexual desire Waltz feels could change to violence without reason or warning. Ruth picks up on the homoerotic element hinted at in the men's being "involved" together when she confronts Nick in scene 3: "Him and that guy with the Martians, they were going to die. / Inside that hole. / What did they *think* of? / When they talked about their broads. / When they were going to die? / You stupid shit. / . . . sucking each other off inside that hole [. . .] there *are* no men" (103). For Nick his father and Waltz represent unknown and perhaps unknowable sources of anxiety and fear: "They had *seen* things [. . .] Who knows. If they were real or not" (40–41). But Ruth insists, "We don't have to be afraid. / Because we have each other" (42).

This might be stated as the moral of Ruth's two major stories, the "Babes in the Woods" story that her grandmother told her and her brother at bedtime and the story of her grandmother's romantic passion with her first husband. The "Babes in the Woods" story contains many standard fairy tale images and tropes. As Ruth says, "there was the moon and wolves and these old women and small children" (54). Grandma tells the children that they can play in the woods, but it is dangerous because of the wolves and bears that live in them, "so we must be careful in the woods. We had to take care of each other, and be very careful not to go too far" (55). The children, of course, become lost and cannot see the moon, but, Ruth says, "I think that always at the end our parents found us in the morning [. . .] Although I don't remember" (56). Connected with these stories are the stories of Cossacks and bears and of people her grandmother helped to escape by hiding them under her petticoats and taking them to safety through the forest (59), a suggestion that female sexuality need not be threatening but may be the salvific counter to the fear that Nick feels about his own sexual drives and desires. Ruth tells, in opposition to the bear, of the blacksmith who was the love of her grandmother's life and an embodiment of powerful male sexuality that, unlike the bear, was unthreatening because it was channeled into romantic passion: "She would tell me, in the Winter, they would make love. Him and her. For hours [. . .] She said he was like Iron. He could lift her in one hand. / They'd lie in bed all day and never speak . . . they'd take long walks" (60). She speaks of the enticing way his "singed forearms" smelled in the rain, taming Nick's fearsome fire imagery with her element of water. Tellingly, she says, "She looked like me" (60), and "She loved him. They were married. / Nothing, even he was crippled—or she was—could separate them. / She was his. Forever. / They had made a vow" (61). Nick says to himself, "Some pagan vow" (61).

The story of the blacksmith is meant to prepare Nick for the gift of the bracelet that Ruth is going to make. Earlier Ruth has told Nick how badly she feels that she has lost the bracelet made from a necklace her grandmother had given her, and she suggests that they could wear rings, bracelets, "long, slim necklaces" wrapped around their wrists "to show that we are lovers" (30). Nick does not respond to this, and his refusal to wear the bracelet she gives him is partly motivated by his fear of entrapment, like the raccoon in the milk container, and partly by his inability to voice or even recognize his feelings for Ruth. When she tells him about the blacksmith, she says it was he who gave his grandmother the necklace: "Can you think, Nick? / All the secrets, all the things they shared? / At night. In bed" (61). Having lost the necklace, her link to her grandmother's experience, Ruth is eager to replicate the symbolism in what she feels is her own great romantic passion for Nick. But Nick is no more the romanticized male of Ruth's fantasies than Ruth is the romanticized female of Nick's. Nick is, at least at the moment, vulnerable, fearful, and, as Christopher Bigsby has suggested, on the edge of hysteria.[27]

It is the "Babes in the Woods" trope that finally applies to Nick and Ruth, as she cradles him in her arms, putting herself in the place of her grandmother as she tells the story: "They lay down [. . .] He put his arms around her [. . .] They lay down in the Forest and they put their arms around each other. / In the dark. And fell asleep" (118). This image of giving and receiving comfort, vividly reminiscent of the ending of O'Neill's *Moon for the Misbegotten*, seems to be the utmost these two are able to achieve in terms of human con-nection. Neither can fulfill the romantic fantasies that the other has of a romantic partner, fantasies that Mamet would certainly ascribe to the same cultural sources that are responsible for the lack of understanding in *Sexual Perversity*. The tragedy is that these two, who, as Ruth insists, have a great deal to give to each other, cannot possibly come together in a mature and committed relationship that is also passionate. They do not have enough knowledge of themselves or of each other. But Mamet has also insisted that the play's tragic trajectory is toward something positive. As he told Bigsby, he sees the play as "about the yearning to commit yourself, to become less deracinated—or more racinated," representing in his career, a movement toward "'a faith in something or other.' Pressed to say what that faith might be, he added, 'a faith in human nature, perhaps.' It is, he insists, 'about change and regeneration not desolation and decay.'" For Mamet the "salvation in that play" is that Nick, who is "trying to live in a rational world, is dragged kicking and screaming into some kind of emotional maturity."[28]

CHAPTER 5

Parents and Children

Mamet's most personal and autobiographical plays, about parents and children, are written from the viewpoint of the child; this is especially true of *The Cryptogram* (1994) and of *Jolly*, the second of the three short plays that make up *The Old Neighborhood* (1997). But even in his earliest writing about the family, *Reunion* and its brief companion piece, *Dark Pony*, there are hints of Mamet's personal experience. *Reunion* suggests the relationship between Mamet's father, Bernard, and his younger sister, Lynn. The forthright Lynn Mamet told an interviewer that, although David grew up admiring their father, "she always hated him."[1] While David left the house of his mother and stepfather to live with his father and stepmother during his teens, Lynn remained there despite the emotional and physical abuse that David depicts in the essay "The Rake" and in the autobiographical *Jolly*.

Reunion, 1976

Reunion is about the meeting of a father and daughter, now aged 53 and 24, who have not seen each other since the daughter was a small child. Mamet calls the father Bernie, his own father's name, and assigns the blame for the estrangement to him, an alcoholic with two failed marriages and a son from whom he is also estranged. Interestingly Carol, his daughter, is David Mamet's age, born in 1947. The meeting has been initiated by Carol, who has tracked down her father through Alcoholics Anonymous and sent her husband, Gerry, to make contact with Bernie at the restaurant where he works.

The play is a series of fourteen short scenes that take place during their meeting in Bernie's apartment, as Bernie and Carol try to find a meeting ground as father and daughter. Bernie's advice to Carol is blunt—she is responsible for making her own happiness: "You got to grab it. / You got to know it and you got to want it. / And you got to *take* it."[2] Bernie is not an amoral social Darwinist, however. He subscribes to a morality of actions and consequences, lessons he has learned by hard experience, and he tries to pass on its rules to his daughter:

> You wanna drink? Go drink.
> You wanna do *this*? Pay the price.
> Always the price. Whatever it is.
> And you gotta know it and be prepared to pay it if you don't
>   want it to pass you by.
> And if you don't know that, you gotta find it out, and that's
>   all I know. (24)

But that is not all Bernie knows. One other principle he tries to pass on to Carol is to live day by day in the moment, for "actions are important / The present is important" (36). As Bigsby has pointed out, the radical simplification of his life that Bernie has achieved, and the practice of taking one day at a time, is a lesson he would have learned in AA.[3] All these are useful pieces of wisdom for Carol, who is unhappy in her current life with her kindhearted husband, Gerry, an older man she respects but is not attracted to, a father substitute.

Edward J. Esche has viewed *Reunion* as a portrait of paternal failure, and Bernie and Carol as two characters who exhibit unrelieved loneliness and pain.[4] While there is no doubt of Mamet's moral stance on responsibility— Bernie's insistence that you have to pay the price—there is more to the play and the meaning of Bernie and Carol's encounter than just that. Although there are rocky moments in the reunion, when their natural resentment and bitterness come to the surface, the play's overall tone is one of conciliation rather than despair. Bernie's advice to Carol is an articulation of part of the play's meaning. The price for the past must be paid in current suffering, guilt, and remorse. But this does not preclude happiness in the future if one is willing to seize the opportunity and act. This is what Bernie and Carol are trying to do, and the ending suggests that they have found a ground on which to build in their mutual desire to be a father and daughter. In traditional comic form the play ends with the anticipation of a celebratory dinner, including not only Bernie and Carol, but Gerry as well, an imperfect but willing family group. Bernie gives Carol a bracelet that he says he found on a bus but has had engraved, "To Carol from her Father," with the wrong date, a suggestion of the flawed relationship that they have the chance to mend by their future actions. Despite the superficial flaw, Carol notes that the bracelet is "real gold," and the play ends with her comment that "the bracelet's lovely" (41) and Bernie's thanks. Symbolizing the family with this flawed but golden circle, Mamet suggests that the future will be better for the actions that Carol, Gerry, and Bernie have taken toward greater human connection.

Dark Pony, 1977

The short one-act play *Dark Pony* was produced with *Reunion* for the first time at Yale Repertory Theatre in 1977, with the actors who played Bernie and Carol, Michael Higgins and Lindsay Crouse, David Mamet's future wife, playing a father and his young daughter in a car, returning home from somewhere. The father tells the daughter the story of an "Indian Brave," Rain Boy, and his friend, Dark Pony, who saves him from a pack of wolves that has encircled him. At the end of the story, the little girl says that she knows they are almost home because she knows the sound of the road. Most spectators and critics have seen this play as a representation of the early relationship of Bernie and Carol, a time before Carol's home was "broken," when Bernie could provide her with a sense of absolute security. Michael Hinden has suggested that, "in the context of Mamet's oeuvre, this moment is a version of paradise regained: a picture of a secure relationship, an intimate voice telling a story in the night [. . .] a satisfying return to home, and the message of the story itself, which promises the child that her powerful, loyal companion (Dad / Dark Pony) will always be there when needed."[5] In the context of *Reunion,* of course, this moment is bittersweet, for it is a reminder of what Carol and Bernie have lost and will never regain, at least not in the same way. As part of "paying the price," Carol will never be able to give Bernie the unwavering trust she gave him as a child, and the safe haven of home has proven to be a chimera. The hope of *Reunion* is that they are on the road to finding another way for them to be father and daughter.

Jolly, 1997

Although *Reunion* and *Dark Pony* are suggestive of Mamet's childhood, *Jolly,* the middle play of the three that make up *The Old Neighborhood* (1997), is directly autobiographical. Mamet's sister Lynn told a *New York Times* reporter that "it was as if David had replayed six or eight of our phone conversations" in writing the play.[6] When asked if *The Old Neighborhood* was a memory play looking back to his childhood, Mamet said, "Well, yeah. *The Old Neighborhood* is kind of a companion piece to the play I did before called *The Cryptogram,* both of which deal with a situation, a domestic situation. *Cryptogram* deals with it in the present, forty years ago. And *The Old Neighborhood* deals with it retrospectively."[7] Leslie Kane has discussed *Jolly* as a memory play, suggesting that "here the memories evoke little laughter and immense pain. With the barest brushstrokes Mamet paints a picture of divorced parents, stepparents, and siblings, of resentments, jealousy, preferential treatment, and mostly the cold reality that the memories and experiences of siblings sharply differ."[8]

In fact *Jolly* evokes the most famous of American memory plays, Tennessee Williams's *The Glass Menagerie*. Like the Williams figure Tom, *Jolly's* Bobby Gould revisits his childhood with a great deal of guilt and remorse about his sister. When Mamet in his early teens left the house of his mother and stepfather to live with his father, Lynn, three years younger, was left behind to suffer the brunt of the emotional and physical abuse from her stepfather and her mother as well. In the play Bobby has come to visit his sister as part of his trip "back to the old neighborhood," an attempt to gain some emotional equilibrium during the breakup of his own marriage.

Bob expresses regret that he has neglected Jolly recently, but the current of his guilt runs deeper than this recent neglect. Jolly expresses resentment toward him for having left her behind many years earlier. When they disagree about their stepbrother and stepsister, Jolly says, "You weren't there." Bob replies, "I was there for part of it," and she comes back at him, "NO. You weren't there, you know. You weren't there. *I* was there. I see where it all comes from."[9] When he says they treated her "like filth," she responds, "Yes. They did. They treated me like filth. Do you know, you don't know, 'cause you weren't there" (48), and she goes on to tell the story of her mother's emotional abandonment of her at the age of ten, in favor of her new stepsister. In the first of the three scenes, Jolly mostly vents her anger to Bob, first about the latest injuries she has suffered from her stepfamily and then about her childhood, incidents that Bob is not aware of and for which he mainly serves as a sounding board. This scene ends with the exchange:

BOB: *Your* problem is: You could not face the fact. They didn't love you.
    And that's your problem. That they did not love us. (*Pause*)
JOLLY: They loved *you*, Buub. (61)

In the second scene, which takes place in the middle of the night, the brother and sister revisit some of the painful scenes of their childhood together, finding in their shared sense of solidarity a basis from which to judge and laugh at the behavior of the adults who had tortured them in adolescence. Jolly finds the strength to say "*fuck* them. Fuck the *lot* of them" (75) for their superior attitude toward her husband, Carl, but, in an anecdote about her fury at a man who reminded her of her stepfather, she also reveals that she is in a constant state of unresolved anger from her childhood. She does, however, express her unconditional love and loyalty for Bob: "I WANT ONE THING. And that is: The thing that is best for you. Period. Paragraph. And the rest of the world can go to hell. I don't give a fuck. I'm too old" (76).

The brief final scene embodies a resolution of sorts for both Jolly and Bob. Jolly tells her brother a recurrent dream that she has mentioned earlier but put off describing in detail. In the dream the stepfamily is knocking on her door, trying to get in, and she knows they want to kill her. Then she hears her mother's voice: "from just beyond the door: 'Julia, Let Me In.' 'I will not let them hurt you . . .' the sweetest voice. 'You are my *child* . . .' and it goes on. 'I won't let them hurt you, darling . . . you are my *child*. You are my *child*. Open the door. Oh. *Julia*. I will not let them Hurt You. OH. My Dear . . .' I open the door, this sweetest voice, and there is *Mom*, with this *expression* on her face . . . (*Pause*) And she wants to kill me. (*Pause*) [. . .] and I knew that she did. So why did I open the door . . . ? (*Pause*) Isn't that the thing of it" (84).

Bob's response, "Thank God it was only a dream" (84), clearly evokes a family cliché for dismissing the children's nightmares. Jolly responds with irony, "Yes. (*Pause*) Isn't that a mercy . . . ?" (84), expressing the knowledge that she understands the dream's significance and can now face the truth about her mother. The brother and sister have shared an experience of revisiting the pain of their childhood, culminating in a moment of deep intimacy. When her husband, Carl, enters, he sees Jolly's emotional state and asks if she would like him to stay home. Her response shows that she no longer feels that Bob deserted her: "No. Thank you. Bobby will be here a while, you see. And he's the only one who knows. (*Pause*) 'Cause he was *there*" (85).

In his memory play Mamet gave Bob a sense of exoneration by his sister that Tennessee Williams never allowed to Tom. Talking to Carl, Jolly and Bob play with the idea that they have been bad and have to make "A Complete and Contrite Apology" (85), but that in a sense is what Bob, and David Mamet, have done for their sisters. The neglect was not only remiss, but criminal. Still Bob does *know*, and he is willing to embrace that knowledge along with his sister so that both of them can find a way to live and raise a family with some measure of emotional comfort.

The Cryptogram 1994

Although *Jolly* focuses on the sister's memories, *The Cryptogram* (1994) deals with events "in the present, forty years ago,"[10] from the point of view of the brother. Mamet was eleven years old when his parents divorced, a year older than John, the character whose point of view defines the audience's experience in *The Cryptogram*. As Mamet expressed it, "I had all this stuff about the kid not going to sleep, and it finally occurred to me, about the billionth draft, well, it's about why can't the kid sleep? It's not that the kid can't sleep but why can't the kid sleep; So, the kid can't sleep because he knows, subconsciously, that something's unbalanced in the household, well then why is nobody paying attention to him? I thought Aha! Well, this is perhaps the question of the play."[11] In writing the play, he said, he thought of the Cryptogram as "a message in code. I guess my idea was that the, that memory is a message in code, like a dream is a message in code, and also a play is a message in code. And [as] one grows up, gets into middle-age, one can look back and try to decode the message of one's childhood, for example, as in the case of this play."[12]

Mamet is also on record as calling *The Cryptogram* one of his four "classically structured tragedies,"[13] along with *Oleanna, American Buffalo,* and *The Woods,* and he has said that "every tragedy's based on deception; that's the meaning of the, the tragic form [. . .] something has been hidden and can only be uncovered, uncovered at great expense. And when it is uncovered we say, 'Oh my gosh, it was in front of me the whole time.'"[14] This deception and uncovering is central to *The Cryptogram's* action. A key to uncovering the meaning of the cryptogram, the play and puzzle, lies in John's dialogue with his mother, Donny, at the beginning of the third act. She tells him, "Things occur. In our lives. And the meaning of them . . . the *meaning* of them . . . is not clear [. . .] But we assume they have a meaning. We must. And we don't know what it is."[15] The action of the play is John's attempt to understand the meaning of what the adults are doing and saying. The audience is engaged in the same quest, while it is simultaneously focused on the effect of these actions on John, "the dynamics of a soul murder," as John Lahr puts it.[16]

The Cryptogram opens with a conversation between John and a man the audience would assume is his father, about his slippers and his inability to sleep. It soon emerges that Del is not John's father, but a family friend, and that John is eagerly anticipating a trip to the woods with his father, Robert, the next day. Both Del and John's mother, Donny, are agitated and distracted, however, and more intent on getting John to go upstairs to bed than on finding out what is wrong with him. At the end of act 1, John finds an envelope that turns out to be a note to Donny from Robert, telling her that he is leaving her. Act 2, the next night, begins with John's deeply troubled questioning of his own and the world's reality as his mother once again tries to get him to go upstairs to bed. Del comes in after an apparently futile search for Robert, and it emerges that Del has lied to Donny about his supposed camping trip with Robert the previous week and instead he has allowed Robert to use his room to meet a woman. Donny throws him out of her house. John comes downstairs to tell his mother about a dream in which he sees a candle in his room from the outside and is "perfectly alone" (44). His mother sends him back to bed.

In act 3, a month later, the house has been packed up in preparation for a move. It opens with John's asking his mother if she ever wished that she could die, saying twice, "It's not such a bad feeling. (*Pause*) Is it?" (45). Donny tells him "You must go to sleep. If you do *not* sleep, *lay* there. Lay in bed. What you think about there is your concern. No one can help you" (51). Del brings gifts that he hopes will earn forgiveness, but they turn out to be worthless because he is mistaken about their sentimental value. John goes upstairs, searching for a blanket he had found in the attic earlier and comes down to get Donny's permission to take it from the box it is packed in, permission which she gives on his promise to go to bed and not come back downstairs. After John leaves, Del tries to get Donny to forgive him, calling himself "some poor Queen [. . .] some silly old Soul Who loves you" (53). Donny refuses, saying that he has betrayed her like every other man she knows and calling him "fairy" and "faggot" (54). Del counters by telling her she provokes betrayal, and he is about to tell her something about her "and the boy" (54) that he has observed for a long time when John appears and Donny erupts in anger over his broken promise to stay upstairs, saying "go away. You lied [. . .] I love you, but I can't like you" (55). John says that he has to cut the twine on the box in order to get the blanket, and Del gives the boy a knife that Robert had given him. As John ignores her commands to say goodnight to Del, Donny demands of her son, "Can't you see that I need comfort? Are you blind? For the love of God" (56). Apologizing to her at Del's insistence, John takes the knife and heads up the stairs, saying that he hears voices calling his name (57).

As John Lahr suggested, in a review that Mamet appreciated so much that he sent him a cast gift, "psychological truth is never acknowledged [in the play]. In fact it is scrambled—like a cryptogram—so that everything means something else."[17] The terms of the cryptogram are to be read in the words the characters speak—the lies and the double-talk that Del and Donny speak to John and to each other, but the key elements are the objects, overdetermined metaphors that are packed with "meaning" and yet are scrambled to make decoding them difficult for both John and the audience.[18]

The most conspicuous object on the set of *The Cryptogram* is the staircase, the only thing besides the couch and the door to the kitchen that Mamet prescribes in the stage directions. The staircase was the dominant element in both the original production in London and the New York production directed by Mamet, in which, as Michael Feingold wrote, the staircase seemed "to stretch up to a dark infinity; the son's last slow ascent of it [. . .] makes the audience gasp [. . .] intensely."[19] Mamet's set evokes one of the classic plays about American childhood, William Inge's *The Dark at the Top of the*

Stairs (1958), also dominated by the stairs. As might be expected in the context of the 1950s, in Inge's play the threat from the stairs is sexual. The danger to the family there is in the too intense Oedipal connection between the mother and her ten-year-old son. During the course of the play, she comes to realize that this intense bond is not good either for him or for her marriage.

Mamet's vision is much darker, of course. His staircase is a liminal space between the living room—where John is being forced to try to understand the loss of his father, the collapse of his family network, his own increasing sense of lost identity and mortality, and the deceitfulness of the adults around him—and the attic, where the totemic objects representing the family's life together are stored. In act 1 Donny sends John up to "close up the attic" (12) as a remedy for his sleeplessness, and Del comments, "*Good*. One sends him up to the Attic [. . .] And that's 'it.' That's the solution" (14). This is on a par with Donny's wishing that she were a monk, "an old man for example [. . .] and all his sons are gone" (17). They want to relegate the child to the attic along with the disturbing memories of the past. But when John comes down into the living room, he is wrapped in the blanket, which embodies Donny's emotional history with Robert and him. She and Robert bought the blanket in England during World War II, and they took it with them on long walks in the country. They used it to cover them when they rather callously made love in front of Del while they were on hikes together. It was used as a coverlet "to keep you warm" (28), as John says, and he was wrapped in it as a baby. The blanket is the focus of John's current anxiety because he thinks it is he who has torn it, even though Donny tries to tell him that "we tore that long ago" (19). When John asks why they stopped using it, Donny says, "we put it away [. . .] it was torn" (29).

The torn blanket is the second of the "three misfortunes" that are in John's mind the equivalent of the three misfortunes in the book about the Wizard, a book whose significance is shared by all three characters. In the book the first two misfortunes carry obvious sexual meanings: "the Lance was broken by the Lord of Night, the Chalice was burnt" (21), thus the male and female principles have been destroyed. In John's reading of his family, the misfortunes are Donny's breaking of the teapot, an obvious maternal symbol, with its implications of the womb, and the tearing of the blanket, the fabric of the family. Despite Donny's attempts to get him to "absolve" (21) himself because the blanket was torn in the past, John continues to feel guilt; he even insists that "something could have been the Third Misfortune, even though it had happened quite long ago [. . .] if, when it *happened*, no one *noticed* [. . .] or neglected to *count* it [. . .] until we recognized it *now*" (23). Mamet plays with the notion of the Third Misfortune when he introduces the stock device of melodrama at the end of the first act, the sudden appearance of the letter saying that Robert has left Donny. But, of course, it is not so simple as this.

The most significant and ominous object on the set of *The Cryptogram* is the male equivalent of Donny's teapot, Robert's "pilot's knife" from World War II. As his essay "Knives" in *Jafsie and John Henry* eloquently shows, David Mamet has been fascinated by knives since his childhood. In his essay "Wabash Avenue," he recorded in detail his first serious purchase of a knife, "advertised as the knife that Francis Gary Powers was carrying when his U2 was shot down over Russia. I don't know why, but that seemed, and still rather seems, a legitimate endorsement."[20] In the play the knife is first introduced when John needs something to cut the twine on the tackle box to get the green fishing line that Robert calls special because "it's very strong" (16), an overt symbol of the ties that bind father and son. Del gives him Robert's knife with which to cut it, and when John's mother questions whether his father would have thought it was all right for him to have the knife, John insists "no, he *would*" (20), and Del gives it to him.

The knife becomes the focus of the tension between John and Del for Robert's love and attention. Del tells Donny that John's resentment over Robert's giving him the knife is evidence of the boy's jealousy of his supposed camping trip with Robert. In act 2, before she knows about the lie Del has told her, Donny tells Del that Robert's gift of the pilot's knife was the "Odd Gesture" telling him that he was leaving her, and Del understands that "when he was forced to *abandon* his . . . (*Pause.*) He looked for *safety*, and the knife, it cut. . . . It 'released' him" (38). It is the knife that reveals Del's lie, in another melodramatic disclosure, when Donny says that Robert could not have given it to Del on their camping trip, because she saw it in the attic afterward, and Del is forced to confess that Robert gave him the knife later, "to shut me up" (42). When he returns in act 3, he brings the knife as "a propitiation. To the boy" for having wronged him (48). To hurt Del, Donny tells him that the knife was not a cherished war memento, but something Robert bought on the street in London, and Del finally realizes that "it had no meaning for him" (50), thus emptying the knife of its heavy symbolic freight.

The final turn of the screw comes at the end of the play. In act 3 Del realizes that the knife, which he had brought to John as a propitiation, is no fit gift for a child, and he offers instead his copy of the Wizard book to read if the boy cannot sleep. John, however, insists that he has to have the blanket, which is tied up in a box in the attic, and Del finally hands him the knife, telling him to "take the knife and go" (57). The meaning of this gesture is not immediately evident. Is it simply indicative of Del's self-absorbed obtuseness that he would hand this disturbed child a knife that he has just said was a dangerous gift in order to get him out of the way? Or does he have a darker motive, intending for the boy to take the knife and do himself harm? This mystery is tied in with the meaning of John's actions. One could see Del's giving him his father's knife as an empowering gesture, especially if it is the means to cut through the Gordian knot in the attic that has kept him from getting to the blanket, with its implications of safety, warmth, and love. Other clues are deeply ominous, however. John keeps telling his mother that he hears voices calling him, and, combined with his guilt, his fear of abandonment, and his thoughts about the loss of identity and death, his last lines as he climbs the staircase to the attic suggest that he will harm himself: "They're calling my name. (*Pause*.) Mother. They're calling my name" (57).

The production that Mamet directed suggested the darker implications for most reviewers. John Lahr recalled the final scene of the London production: "At the finale, John is looking down over the bannister at Donny and Del. He flicks the knife. The blade jolts into view with a startling *thwack*—a chilling sound that holds out the promise, as the lights fade, of murderous fury directed at John himself or at the world."[21] Michael Feingold has noted the audience's audible gasp as John slowly climbed the stairs in the Mamet's production.[22]

If *The Cryptogram* begins with a visual allusion to Inge's play, it ends, as Jill Gidmark has noted, with an allusion to Ibsen's equally disturbing treatment of childhood, *The Wild Duck*, in which "a child secretly takes off to an attic bearing a pistol, her anticipated suicide the consequence of chilling games that the adults in her house play."[23] If the outcome, the answer to the cryptogram, remains ultimately hidden, this is clearly part of the "coded message" of the play that Mamet expects the audience to read. It is difficult to imagine anything like the happy resolution of Inge's play happening for Donny, Del, and John.

CHAPTER 6

Confidence Games

The simplest definition of a confidence game is a swindle in which the con artist defrauds the victim, or "mark," of money by first gaining the mark's confidence or trust. As Susan Kuhlmann has pointed out, the confidence game is as old in English literature as Chaucer's Pardoner and Canon. Most literary historians consider the first important representation of the American confidence man to be Johnson Jones Hooper's *Simon Suggs* (1845), famous for his credo, "It's good to be shifty in a new country." The con artist's literary apotheosis is generally seen to be Frank Goodman in Melville's *The Confidence Man: His Masquerade* (1857), but several studies have shown that the con artist, both male and female, was very much alive in U.S. literature throughout the twentieth century.[1]

Mamet is one of the confidence game's most devoted students. His work reflects his perennial fascination with confidence games and con artists. In essays he has written about the time he spent hanging around Chicago pool halls in his youth, observing "the short con," the swindle that can be completed in one sitting. As he wrote in *Writing in Restaurants*, "the point of the pool hall was the intersection of two American Loves: the Game of Skill and the Short Con. The denizens of the pool hall came in to practice their skill, and the transients were those upon which the skill was practiced."[2] In interviews he has talked about the jobs he held in shady sales operations in his early manhood. He has had a long friendship and working collaboration with magician and card sharp Ricky Jay, who has appeared in several of Mamet's films and can currently be seen showcasing his card tricks on YouTube.

Mamet's intense interest in the art of the con has led to several intricately wrought plays and movie scripts based on confidence games, such as *House of Games*, *The Spanish Prisoner*, *The Shawl*, and *Heist*. In early plays such as

The Water Engine and *Edmond,* Mamet not only incorporated confidence games into his plots, but he constructed a reality that is deeply informed by the dynamics of the con game and reflective of a moral and social universe that sees every human transaction in terms of confidence man and mark, a reality that is more fully developed in his plays of the mid-1980s, *Glengarry Glen Ross* and *Speed-the-Plow,* where everyone is conning everyone else all the time. The defining principle of the characters' lives might be Mamet's well-known description of the American businessman's creed, "hurray for me and to hell with you."[3]

Mamet's conception of the confidence game is knowledgeable and precise. His understanding of the psychological complexities of the con artist and the mark is particularly evident in *House of Games,* but it informs all of the work that is based on this relationship. His construction of the con artist reflects what John Blair calls the identifying ploy of the confidence man, that he cheats "only those who are themselves ready to cheat." A con man "offers his victim partnership in an illegal scheme, the more sure because it is illicit. The victim must agree in advance to participate in trickery."[4] This sense of the mark's double identity, that he is simultaneously the exploited and the would-be exploiter, has fascinated Mamet, but he is perhaps more interested in the moral universe pervaded by, and often constructed by, the confidence game. Although he has made thematic, metaphoric, and metonymic use of the con game throughout his career, it was during the 1970s and 1980s, before his renewed interest in his Jewish faith and political identity, that it served him most completely as a metaphor for life in the United States. In the works of this period, it often seems that the only way of beating the "Big Con" that is the life of the characters under the U.S. economic system is a successful short con. The odds of doing this, and the terms on which it can be done, vary greatly from play to play.

The Water Engine, 1977

A good example of the deterministic condition of life under the big con is represented in *The Water Engine: An American Fable,* which Mamet wrote first as a radio play for NPR's anthology series *Earplay* in 1977. The stage version reached Broadway in 1978. In 1992 it was made into a film and shown on television by Turner Broadcasting. Mamet has described the play as "an American fable about the common person and the institution."[5] He stated that "the story starts like this: 'In September 1934, a young man in Chicago, Illinois, designed and built an engine which used distilled water as its only fuel," and it is based on "one of our hardiest and beloved myths [. . .] that of *suppression* by the government, or by an industrial pseudo-government, of discoveries or of inventions which could improve our lives."[6] In a sense the play is a dramatization of Mamet's view of U.S. society in the 1970s.

As is appropriate to the Depression era in which the play is set, the confidence game Mamet employs in *The Water Engine* is the chain letter, a persistent and popular phenomenon in American culture that reached one of its peaks in the mid-1930s. Mamet's play combines the "luck" chain letter, which was popular during the 1920s, with the "prosperity" chain letter that arose during the 1930s. The first type did not ask the recipient to send money, but only promised good fortune if it was passed it on and threatened disaster if he or she failed to do so. The prosperity type instructed the recipient to send money, usually a dime, to the first person on the list, giving the recipient concrete expectations of money rather than the vague hope of prosperity produced by the luck letter. The prosperity chain letter is a confidence game, playing on the recipient's trust and greed. The terms of the con, monetary reward if you follow the instructions and disaster if you do not, are as simple as they come, and the game's popularity is proof of its attraction. In 1935, during the height of the send-a-dime craze, one man in Denver reported receiving 2,363 letters from the chain when he returned from a two-day vacation.[7] The game flourishes in email form on the Internet to this day.

The Water Engine uses the chain letter as one of several layers of theatrical representation. The play is presented as a 1934 radio show about Chicago's Century of Progress Exhibition, which Mamet, a collector of its memorabilia, knew a great deal about. The chain letter is introduced in voiceover, and the story of Charles Lang, who has invented the water engine, is introduced as part of the chain letter. Like the typical luck chain letter, this letter promises that "happiness and health will be yours,"[8] if you pass it on, listing people who received large sums of money for continuing the chain, but it also ascribes Sanford White's murder and the Lindbergh baby's kidnaping to the chain's having been broken. Like the prosperity chain letter, it requires the recipient to send money, in this case a dollar, to the person at the top of the list. In the play Mamet uses the chain letter as a metonym for the American myth as he defines it, "the idea of something out of nothing."[9] To make this metonymic quality clear, he has Lang insist on giving the lawyer Gross, whom he wants to help him secure the patent for his engine, a dollar for a retainer, saying "if I give you money then we have a contract." Gross responds, "then you can trust me. Is that what you're saying?" (14). He takes the dollar, but then he reminds Lang, "if you couldn't trust me what good would your contract be?" (14).

The contract proves to be no good at all, for, once Gross is convinced that the engine works, he turns Lang over to the sinister Oberman, the lawyer for unnamed corporate interests who tries to get Lang to sell them the engine. They kidnap his sister, who warns him that they will not make the engine but destroy the plans if they get them. When it becomes clear that the police and the press are in league with Oberman, Lang sees little hope, and indeed he and his sister end up as "mutilated bodies" found on a stretch of industrial lake frontage. But Lang has sent the plans forward, like a chain letter, to Bernie, a young boy who may be able to build the engine some day.

Having told his story to a friendly barker at the fair, Charles has not broken the chain. The chain letter says that "one man saw the plans for a machine which he was told would run on water as its only fuel" (60), indicating that the barker has passed on the story along with a chain letter he received. The greatest hope, of course, resides in the boy, Bernie, who has the talent to one day realize the plans for the engine that he will receive in the mail. But what does this signify? Presumably, building the engine will prove as disastrous for Bernie as it has for Lang. Mamet has said that the theme of *The Water Engine* comes down to the chain letter's message that "All people are connected."[10] But that is not necessarily a good thing. It depends on what that connection serves. The chain letter is a confidence game, after all. If it only serves Oberman's paraphrase of Adam Smith, that "if everyone just acted in his own best interests this would be a paradise on earth" (39), the play implies that the connectedness of corporate interests, the state, and the media only combines to make a hell on earth, not a paradise. They combine to inhibit humankind's progress while praising it to the skies. On the other hand, there is the individual, represented by the "little people," the Langs, the barker, and Bernie and his father. Their interests are in the community. They help each other. But they are no match for the real powers in this society. *The Water Engine* is a dark play. Like the film noir that the motion picture version effectively imitates, it presents a dark and threatening world to its everyman protagonist, and though, like much thirties literature, it offers communal interests as a hope against the economic and social forces the individual is up against, that hope is at best a dim one.

Glengarry Glen Ross, 1983

Glengarry Glen Ross is Mamet's most devastatingly direct treatment of U.S. business. Discussing the play in an interview with Matthew Roudané, he alluded to Thorstein Veblen's concept from the *Theory of the Leisure Class* that "sharp practice inevitably shades over into fraud. Once someone has no vested interest in behaving in an ethical manner and the only bounds on his behavior are supposedly his innate sense of fair play, then fair play becomes an outdated concept."[11] Mamet locates the origin of this condition squarely within the idea of the American Dream. "The national culture is founded very much on the idea of strive and succeed. Instead of rising with the masses, one should rise from the masses. Your extremity is my opportunity. That's what forms the basis of our economic life, and this is what forms the rest of our lives. That American myth: the idea of something out of nothing. And this also affects the spirit of the individual. It's very divisive. One feels one can only succeed at the cost of someone else."[12] This attitude of course is also what informs the mentality of the con game, the paradigmatic game in which fair play is an outdated concept. In *Glengarry Glen Ross,* Mamet represents the business practices in a real estate office engaged in selling worthless undeveloped land by using a series of sale pitches, each of which is a miniconfidence game that plays on the trust, the greed, and the weaknesses or emotional vulnerability of the mark to get something for nothing, or as close to it as possible.

Mamet was well prepared to write this play by two jobs he had as a young man in Chicago in the late 1960s. One was selling carpet over the telephone, "cold calling out of the blue book, absolutely cold."[13] Asked by John Lahr in 1997 if he remembered his sales pitch, he launched into a creditable telephone spiel but admitted that he was a terrible salesman: "I kept identifying with the people on the other end, which is something you really can't do."[14] The other job was in 1969, when he was just out of college, working for a year in "a boiler room [. . .] trying to sell people worthless land in Arizona and Florida. You follow up leads, like responses to a TV ad or something like that, and make appointments so a salesman can go out and seal the deal."[15] Years later he expressed the guilt he felt for selling "worthless land to elderly people who couldn't afford it"[16] He told another interviewer, "I was in charge of the leads, like the character [Williamson] in *Glengarry Glen Ross.*"[17] Writing the play clearly drew on Mamet's inside knowledge of the real estate business and experience with telephone sales, and it also served as expiation for his participation in it. The idea for the play's form he ascribed to his habit of listening to conversations when he was in restaurants: "There's nothing more fascinating than the people in the next booth. You start in the middle of the conversation and wonder, What the hell are they talking about?"[18]

In form *Glengarry Glen Ross* is simple. Act 1, set in a Chinese restaurant, consists of three scenes, in three separate booths, each an exchange between a salesman and someone he is trying to convince to do something. Act 2, set in the real estate office where the salesmen work, consists of one scene in which the outcomes of the act 1 exchanges manifest themselves and affect one other. The play's epigraph is "Always Be Closing," which Mamet identifies as a "practical sales maxim" in the script.[19] A number of critics have pointed out that, for these men who make their living with their sales pitches, language is action. David Worster has discussed the play in terms of speech-act theory, noting that, in the play, "the primary purpose of utterance is not to communicate, but to claim power or to withhold it from others," and Jonathan S. Cullick has noted that "each scene is a locus of persuasion, and the subtext of a sales pitch conditions (or informs) every interaction."[20] Robert Vorlicky's extensive discussion of the play's social dialogue is based on the idea that "the social dialogue in *Glengarry* is dramatic talk that is 'always closing,' as it were, not only because of its limited selection of topics (its nearly exclusive, closed focus on one's job) but in its conversational dynamic between participants."[21]

Each of the three scenes in act 1 is in fact composed of a sales pitch. The background context that emerges is that the office is having a sales contest in which the salesman with the highest sales volume gets a Cadillac, the one with the second highest gets a set of steak knives, and the two with the lowest lose their jobs. An older salesman, Shelly "The Machine" Levene, the former star of the office whose sales have fallen off, is trying to get the young office manager, Williamson, to break the office rules and give him the new "premium leads," or sales prospects, so he can finally close a sale and keep his job. In the second scene Dave Moss, the second-highest-performing salesman, tries to convince George Aaronow, whose job is in jeopardy, to stage a robbery of the office, steal the new leads, and sell them to the firm's competitor Jerry Graff, who supposedly will give him a sales job in return. In the third scene Richard Roma, the first-place salesman, is running his sales pitch on James Lingk, someone he met in the restaurant. Each of these verbal transactions is a sales pitch of sorts and, as part of the whole shady real estate operation, which sells virtually worthless land to people who think they will make a big profit by turning it over, is also a con game. Each of the men uses the techniques of the confidence game to draw in the mark and get him to give him what he wants.

In the first scene the audience is shown why Levene is not closing his sales. In an unmistakable allusion to Miller's *Death of a Salesman*, Levene, like Willy Loman, tries to talk his young boss into letting him keep his job by reminding him of his past accomplishments, and he assumes they will continue to define him. "Put a *closer* on the job [. . .] put a *proven man out*" (15), he tells Williamson. Like Willy's boss, however, Williamson refuses to buy into Levene's nostalgic and exaggerated account of his past glory, parrying every claim with a harsh dose of reality. When he sees that reminders of his past success are not working, Levene shifts to playing on Williamson's self-interest. He offers him a bribe of 10 percent of his sales. Williamson counters with 20 percent, which Levene immediately agrees to, and then Williamson raises the stakes, adding "fifty bucks a lead" (24). Levene tries unsuccessfully to negotiate, offering Williamson thirty dollars, an amount which is refused, and then he falls back on ploys which he should know by now will not work, trying to reach Williamson emotionally by bringing up his daughter and reminding him of the power he had over him in the past. Finally he offers fifty dollars for one lead, but now Williamson refuses to split them. In his attempt to con Williamson into giving him the leads, Levene has been bested at every turn, and it is now Williamson who will benefit from this transaction, assuming that Levene will ever be able to pay him for the leads. The only way he manages to con Williamson is out of a lunch, as he tells him, "you know, I left my wallet back at the hotel" (27).

In the second scene Dave Moss is more skilled at his sales pitch than Levene, more ruthless, and seemingly more effective at getting what he wants. He begins by addressing the essential thing for both confidence games and sales, winning the mark's trust. The scene opens with Moss commiserating with Aaronow over his failure to make a sale to what Moss calls "Polacks and deadbeats" (28). Establishing their comradeship against an ethnic Other, Moss launches into a tirade against Indians, which elides into an attack on Mitch and Murray, the new bosses who have come in to the business and "killed the goose" (30), as Moss says, with their shady tactics. Knowing that Aaronow, unlike the rest of the crew, has moral compunctions about the business, Moss affects a higher moral standard, putting himself in opposition to the new bosses, who think they will "go in and rob everyone blind and go to Argentina cause nobody ever *thought* of this before" (32).

Moss plays on Aaronow's masculine pride as well as his fear, suggesting that Mitch and Murray take "a fuckin' *man,* worked all his *life*" and make him "cower in his boots" (32) with their "sales promotion" (32). Asserting that this is just wrong, he brings up their competitor, Jerry Graff, who is clean and, he says, doing very well with his leads from a list of nurses. Their own leads, Moss says, are the problem, and he challenges Aaronow, saying that what's needed is to be independent as Jerry Graff is, to act. Before he broaches his real subject, Moss has one more rhetorical strategy to deploy. He uses the language of slavery to describe their current situation: "you find yourself in *thrall* to someone else. And we *enslave* ourselves" (35) to please Mitch and Murray. His rhetoric ascends to the level of an emotional defense of salesmen: "when they *build* your business, then you can't fucking turn around, *enslave* them, treat them like *children,* fuck them up the ass, leave them to fend for themselves" (36).

Having established his bond with Aaronow, who has responded positively to his spiel, and positioned the two of them as united in opposition to the oppressive bosses who are ruining the business with their immoral tactics,

Moss is ready to go after what he wants from Aaronow. Someone should strike back, he says, someone should "hurt them" (37), "someone should rob the office" (38). The leap from striking back at the oppressors to robbing the office is Moss's most risky ploy, and when Aaronow accepts it with a simple "Huh." (38), he plunges ahead with his pitch, saying they could break in to the office, make it look like a robbery, take the leads and sell them to Jerry Graff for five thousand dollars. As Aaronow questions him about how much he has talked to Graff about this, Moss equivocates, producing the well-known exchange about whether they are "talking" about the robbery or "just speaking" about it. When Aaronow finally gets Moss to admit that he has presented the idea to Graff, he says that Graff, the "clean" businessman, is ready to offer them five thousand dollars for the leads and give them jobs.

Moss now ups the ante, telling Aaronow that he is the one who has to rob the office, while Moss establishes an alibi for himself, and that he has to do it that night. When Aaronow refuses, Moss comes in for the kill, or the closer. He tells him that he has to do it because, in the eyes of the law, he is already an accessory before the fact. Moss exposes a deeper level of ruthlessness when he tells Aaronow that he lied about the amount of money, implying that he will get more than Aaronow, and ending, "In or out. You tell me, you're out you take the consequences" (46). When Aaronow asks why, Moss says, "Because you listened" (46). At the end of this exchange, Moss seems to have succeeded completely at conning Aaronow into doing the robbery for him. After first gaining his trust and playing on his sense of oppression and his desperate desire for a new job, Moss has proceeded to draw Aaronow into the scheme, getting him to the point where he is so deeply implicated that he seemingly has no choice but to do what Moss wants.

The third scene consists of Ricky Roma's sales pitch to the hapless James Lingk, whom he has met in the bar of the Chinese restaurant. Roma's pitch to Lingk follows the general strategy of the confidence game, but it also bears the stamp of originality befitting the star salesman of the crew. Roma begins with a confession: "all train compartments smell vaguely of shit. It gets so you don't mind it. That's the worst thing that I can confess" (47). As Jon Tuttle has noted, this association of the train car, the metaphor for the life of the salesman, with excrement is an indictment of the whole sales profession.[22] Roma in a sense is saying that he is shit, establishing a bond with Lingk, whom he has already sized up to be a dejected loser, drinking by himself in a Chinese restaurant. Saying that it took him a long time to come to this admission, Roma probes for the specific locus of Lingk's weakness, suggesting that it is possible to rise above being "queer," a "thief," having "cheated on your wife," and even "fuck[ing] little girls" (47). Roma rejects being "befuddled by a middle-class morality," and the idea that "bad people go to hell" (47), instead turning Lingk's attention to a possible way out of his current misery: "A hell exists on earth? Yes. I won't live in it" (47). Sensing Lingk's sexual anxiety, Roma moves on to taboo bodily references that suggest his own sensuality and liberation, and he shares reminiscences of his amorous successes.

Having established himself as a model of free sensual experience unencumbered by morality, Roma heads to his major themes, that one has to seize the moment, to trust oneself (Mamet's nod to Emerson), to "do those things which seem correct to me *today*" (49), and above all to act "*each day* without fear" (49). Investments, he says, are opportunities, events, that can mean what you want them to mean. Security and comfort he dismisses with a vaguely existential reminder of the operation of chance in one's life: "all it is, it's a carnival" (50). Thus he has sized up Lingk as a weak man who is morally troubled by his sexual urges and is offering him a way out by leaving his fears behind, by identifying with Roma, clearly a free man with a great sex life, and by seizing the opportunity to "trust himself" by taking action. The opportunity for action Roma presents to him is in the form of his real estate brochure for Glengarry Highlands. While this sales pitch ends here, in the middle of things, it appears to be successful. Roma has clearly drawn Lingk in by playing on his trust and his vulnerability, and he is ready to close the deal.

In act 2 the outcomes of the three separate exchanges are fused, as it emerges that someone has robbed the office, presumably Aaronow, and that Roma has closed the deal with Lingk. Mamet has drawn the audience into believing in the success of Moss's and Roma's sales pitches. Two more confidence games are introduced in act 2. One is Levene's surprising sale of eight units for eighty-two thousand dollars to Bruce and Harriet Nyborg, which he describes in retrospect, and the other is the confidence game that Roma and Levene work together to keep James Lingk from cancelling his contract within the three business days he is allowed by law. Levene's sales pitch is, as he says, "like in the *old* days [. . .] like I was taught" (73). He has drawn in the Nyborgs with the message to trust themselves, "see that opportunity . . . and *take* it" (72). With the pen in his hand, he has told them that this is the thing they have been dreaming of, "the bag that's full of money" (72), dismissing their fear and their desire to be safe by buying less. Claiming that he sat there for twenty-two minutes in silence until they signed, he says, they "both kind of *imperceptibly slumped*. And he reaches and takes the pen and signs, he passes it to her, she signs" (74). As Anne Dean has suggested, this climax is "almost orgasmic."[23] It is celebrated with a drink, and Shelly proclaims to the other men that he has his "*balls* back" (102). Williamson says, however, that it will be a miracle if the sale sticks, and it later emerges that Williamson had known the Nyborgs were not viable prospects, that he had called the bank to check their credit when the lead came in, and that there is a memo about them, suggesting that he had set Levene up by giving him a lead that he knew was no good. Thus Levene's triumphant sale based on "the old ways" is really another failure and Williamson has pulled a con job on him.

In the second con, Levene, working with Roma, is much more effective. Acting on the cues Roma feeds him, Levene poses as a big-time investor in property who gives Roma the excuse he needs to leave in a hurry so that Lingk will not have time to cancel his contract. When Lingk says that his wife has called the attorney general's office, however, this strategy is abandoned, and Roma resorts to double-talk. He finally tells Lingk that his check had not been cashed, which he thinks is a lie but is actually true. When Lingk apologizes to Roma and confesses that he is caving in to his wife and does not have the power to negotiate, Roma is once again able to gain his confidence. Roma is about to get Lingk out of the office and into a bar when they are interrupted by Williamson and the detective who is investigating the robbery. Thinking he is reassuring Lingk about the robbery, Williamson makes the mistake of volunteering that his contract went out and the check was cashed. This, of course, is a lie as well as a mistake. Telling Roma not to follow him but also apologizing to him for letting him down, Lingk leaves the office. Roma unleashes his fury on Williamson, saying "you stupid fucking *cunt*. You *idiot*. Whoever told you you could work with *men*? [. . .] you never open your mouth till you know what the shot is. (*Pause.*) You fucking *child*" (96–97).

Williamson has been under a good deal of stress throughout act 2. His job is on the line because of the robbery. He has taken abuse from Roma for losing the leads and from Levene for not telling Mitch and Murray about his sale. After the mistake with the contract, not only Roma, but Levene, heaps abuse on him, and, most galling of all, Levene tells him he does not belong in the business and berates him for not knowing that "a man who's your 'partner' *depends* on you . . . you have to go *with* him and *for* him . . . or you're shit, you're *shit*, you can't exist alone" (98). Levene, however, has overreached, and he makes a mistake of his own, telling Williamson, "you're going to make something up, be sure it will *help* or keep your mouth closed" (98). This advice leads Williamson to the knowledge that Levene was the only one who knew the contract was on his desk instead of at the bank and thus that he robbed the office. Ironically Levene has exposed himself by doing just what he is berating Williamson for, failing to keep his mouth shut.

In a shift of the power dynamic, Williamson accuses Levene of robbing the office and cons him by telling him that he will not turn him in if he tells where the leads are. Levene immediately gives in and confesses, and he also gives the lie to all his talk about standing by his partner when he gives up Moss as well. A desperate Levene makes another attempt at a sales pitch, trying to get Williamson not to turn him in. He tries to bribe him, offering him first the twenty-five hundred dollars from the robbery, then 20 percent of his sales, and then raising it to 50. Williamson not only refuses the bribe, but he tells him he is deluded about the sale to the Nyborgs. When Levene asks why he is turning him in, he says, "because I don't like you." A final plea to help his daughter, like the earlier plea in act 1, which received no response, gets only a "Fuck you" (104).

This scene would seem to bring closure to the play, but Mamet is not quite through. Roma pulls one last con. When he comes out of the police interrogation and Williamson goes in, he flatters Levene about his work on the Lingk con, and he says, "there's a man I would work with" (105). When Levene is called in to be interrogated, Roma tells Williamson that his and Levene's sales are now to be put together, but "I GET HIS ACTION. My stuff is *mine,* whatever *he* gets for himself, I'm taking half" (107). This ending was cut from the U.S. premiere of the play, and it does not appear in the film version, but Mamet included it in the published version. The question of its inclusion is important because it determines whether the play ends with the poignant poetic justice of Levene's arrest or with the implication that this amoral world will go on as before, with the constant deals and cons that the men live by, regardless of the fate of one aging salesman. The implications are integral to the play's genre, and therefore its meaning.

Mamet has not been consistent in talking about this issue. In 1986 he distinguished *Glengarry Glen Ross*'s genre from the classical tragedy of *American Buffalo,* suggesting that, "although it has aspects of tragedy in it, [it] is basically a melodrama—or a drama,"[24] and citing the unresolved ending, lacking the classical tragic elements of recognition, reversal, and katharsis, as the fundamental difference. Two years later he was quite insistent about calling the play a "gang comedy," which he defined as "a play about revealing the specific natures and the unifying natures of a bunch of people who happen to be involved in one enterprise,"[25] along the lines of *The Front Page.* At that point, he resisted the idea that the play was a "melodrama with good guys and bad guys,"[26] alluding to the contest between good and evil, with the restoration of the forces of good that usually happens in melodrama.

One clue to the question of whether the play shades toward deeply ironic comedy or melodrama is the character of Aaronow. Mamet said that he is "the one who comes closest to being the character of a *raisonneur,* for throughout the whole play he's saying, 'I don't understand what's going on,' 'I'm no good,' 'I can't fit in here,' 'I'm incapable of either grasping those things

I should or doing those things that I've grasped.' Or his closing lines, 'Oh, God, I hate this job.'"[27] Aaronow, Mamet said, "has some degree of conscience, some awareness; he's troubled. Corruption troubles him,"[28] but Aaronow is confused as to whether his failure to succeed is "a defect—that is, is he manly or sharp enough?—or if it's, in effect, a positive attribute [. . .] that his conscience prohibits him."[29] Aaronow, in other words, as the only character who has a moral sense, embodies the moral dilemma for the audience. What should he do? What do his actions signify? How should we regard them?

As Andrea Greenbaum has pointed out, Aaronow is the only character in the play who is not a liar.[30] He is also the only character with any moral convictions. Despite Moss's skillful con job and the appearance that Aaronow has enmeshed himself inextricably in this crime through the tragic mistake of "listening," he refuses to rob the office. Despite Moss's utter exploitation of him, Aaronow stays true to his word not to turn him in, even in the face of what he calls "*gestapo* tactics" (89) by the police—unlike Levene, who sells Moss out in a heartbeat. In this context, he shows himself to be a courageous and principled man. Yet he continues to believe that he is "no fucking good" (57) because he is unable to close the deals on the worthless real estate properties.

Given what the two characters represent, the ending of the play, with Roma's laying the foundation for his plan to bilk Levene out of half his commissions while Aaronow groans, "Oh, God, I hate this job" (108), suggests a deep comic irony. Roma is perfectly happy to keep the wheels of absolute self-interest turning, and Aaronow has nowhere else to go. In the play's terms, there is no escape from the world of the big con of U.S. business. And there is no real poetic justice in Levene's arrest. In a world rife with corruption, why arrest one man rather than another? Moss will also be caught, but why does Roma go free, or Williamson? The play is comic only in the sense that, in Aaronow's confused but insistent acting on his principles, it gestures toward a better world.

The Shawl, 1985

Expanding on this gesture, two years later Mamet wrote a play that suggests the short con might exist in a world that is not necessarily drained of all morality and human values by the big con. *The Shawl* is a short play that was first produced in April 1985 on a double bill with *The Spanish Prisoner* (a one-act play unrelated to the film of the same name), directed by Gregory Mosher at Chicago's Goodman Theatre. Mosher reprised his production for his opening effort as director of the Lincoln Center theater in December. Most reviewers thought it a rather odd choice for Mosher's debut production at Lincoln Center, "minor Mamet" and nothing like the Mamet they were used to from *American Buffalo* and *Glengarry Glen Ross*. In an interview Mamet's wife at the time, Lindsay Crouse, who played Miss A, said that Mamet began the play partly to answer people who told him that he did not write good plots. She said, "he set out to exercise plot-writing as a craft. And I think it came out beautifully. Everybody gets fooled at least once in this play."[31]

In *The Shawl*, John makes his living by practicing the confidence game of convincing a mark that he is a psychic and then, when he has won her over by helping her "to do whatever it is she wants to do,"[32] he gets her to give him some money "to carry on the work." In the first act John practices his craft on Miss A, who, devastated because her mother has died and left her fortune to her stepfather, is trying to decide whether to contest the will, and perhaps she is hoping to be given some kind of moral or psychological permission to do so. John deftly draws this information from her, first gaining her confidence by telling her that he knows she wants him to prove himself by reading her mind and then persuading her of his powers. In act 2 John explains his technique to his young lover and apprentice, Charles, who, it becomes clear, is impatient with their lack of money and the slow pace of John's operation and is on the verge of leaving him. John explains to him that "it comes down to confidence. They'll *test* you. And you can do nothing till you have their trust" (16). John demonstrates his craft by conning Charles, an act that angers him. The power dynamic shifts, as Charles decides that "we should take her fortune from her" (31) and demands that they hold the seance Miss A wants, to commune with her mother's spirit, giving John the ultimatum that he will leave if John refuses.

Act 3 consists of the seance, as John supposedly channels a spirit guide who makes contact with the mother, who in turn tells Miss A that she should "let this man decide [. . .] be free of the money" (40). In a surprising turn of plot, Miss A exposes John and explodes in anger, saying, "how can you *prey* on me? Is there no *mercy* in the world" (43) and "may you rot in hell, in *prison*, . . . you *charlatan*, you *thief* . . . (44). John calls on God to forgive him and then manages to reconnect with Miss A when he tells her that he has seen her mother singing to her as child and wrapping her in a red shawl, a shawl that she has lost five years previously. In act 4 the tables have turned between John and Charles. Charles is begging to stay with John, and John is telling him he has to go. John explains the shawl vision as a trick based on library research, "perhaps two pictures. Of a woman in a red-fringed shawl" (47). He finally dismisses Charles. Miss A returns and tells John that she is going to contest the will. When she asks about payment, he tells her to give what she can afford "to help us with our work [. . .] it's completely up to you" (52). He tells her that he did see her mother wrap her in the shawl, and that "you did *not* lose it. You *burnt* it. In rage. Standing somewhere by the water, five years ago" (53). When she questions him even further, he says, "That is all I saw" (53).

Many reviewers saw the play as leaving the question of John's vision open. Tish Dace, for example, praised Mike Nussbaum's performance in playing the psychic "who is lying to somebody (either in professing his powers to his client or in denying them to his young gay lover)."[33] Mamet has tipped his hand in suggesting that "the older guy in *The Shawl* wants to teach a lesson to his young lover and ends up experiencing a true psychic vision."[34] In other words he is lying not to Miss A about seeing the shawl, but to Charles, when he explains away his psychic vision. Mamet speaks of his construction of the plot in Aristotelian terms, calling it "a twentieth-century version of the idea that what the hero is following and what he ends up with may be two very different things, but they are nonetheless related in the subconscious [. . .] what happens at the crucial moment, as Aristotle says, is that the protagonist undergoes both recognition of the situation and a reversal of the situation. And that is what strikes the responsive chord in the audience—that what is revealed to have been the low objective is transmogrified into the high objective. And we realize that the high objective is carried in the low objective all the time."[35]

The psychic vision works for John as a true realization. Put to the test, he is not, in his soul, a con man, whose fundamental goal must be to bilk this woman out of her fortune without reference to morality or sentiment. This is the reason he must dismiss Charles, who is fully capable of doing so. In fact John wants to help Miss A, as he, in his way, helps the others who come to him. He does this not through psychic powers, but by freeing them to do "whatever it is [they want] to do" (20), which is what he does in giving Miss A permission to contest her mother's will. When John returns to the terms of his old con game, inviting her to leave whatever amount of money she wishes, it is with the confidence that in a sense he has earned this money. He has helped Miss A, and this is what he wants to do, despite the fact that he is a charlatan. When asked whether John has "some sort of moment of intense clarity," Mamet responded, "Yes, I think so."[36]

Confidence Women

Although Mamet depicts the confidence game primarily as a realm of men, he has created several female con artists who not only play with the men, but occasionally beat them. Margaret Ford, in Mamet's 1987 film *House of Games*, is the most fully developed of these characters, and Mamet's work with that film certainly made his more lighthearted treatment of the characters

Karen in *Speed-the-Plow* and Anna in *Boston Marriage* possible. Margaret is the clear winner in *House of Games*. She not only cons Mike; she destroys him, and she frees herself from her father's moral condemnation of her to achieve what seems to be the same amorality that allows the con men to prosper in the game.

Speed-the-Plow, 1988

Like *House of Games, Speed-the-Plow* places a seemingly naive woman, Karen, in the position of initiate into an exclusive male game, in this case, the motion picture business. It also has multiple layers of plot. While Bobby Gould, who has just been promoted to head of production at a motion picture studio, is the protagonist, he is acted on by the two other characters, Charlie Fox, who has come to offer him the boon of a prison buddy film starring Doug Brown, the most bankable star in Hollywood, in exchange for a producing credit, and Karen (no surname), a temporary secretary who wants to get into the movie business. Bob makes a big point of the fact that Charlie, his old friend and subordinate, has been loyal to him in bringing him the offer, when he could easily have "gone across the street" to another studio and perhaps been executive producer of the movie. Bob sets out to con Karen, as he makes a bet with Charlie that he can get her to his house and into bed that night. He offers her the chance to report on "The Bridge: or, Radiation and the Half-Life of Society. A Study of Decay,"[37] a book about the end of the world by a Very Famous Eastern Writer, which Bobby has been told to give a courtesy read by the studio head Ross, who, Bobby knows, has no intention of making such a movie because no one will come to see it. Karen jumps at the chance and agrees to his suggestion that she bring her report on the book to his house that night. When she does, in act 2, she argues passionately that Bobby should make the film because the book is a work of art that will change people, as it has changed her, and will bring hope and love to the world. In act 3, the next day, Bob tells Charlie he is going to make the radiation film instead of the buddy film, and Charlie and Karen enact their own contest, or agon, as each of them tries to get Bobby to produce his or her movie.

The battle emerges as a contest between degrading entertainment in the buddy film, which is replete with violence, blood, racism, and homophobia, and faux "Art" in the "satirically lugubrious *Bridge*,"[38] which is unmasked on stage as the characters read pretentiously nonsensical passages from it. At the crisis point Charlie exposes Karen's motives when he gets her to admit that she would not have slept with Bobby if he had said no to greenlighting the *Bridge* project. Despite the fact that he complains constantly that everyone around him is interested only in getting him to make a film, Bobby was convinced that Karen had sex with him because she likes him (37). When she admits that she was doing what all the "Old Whores" in Hollywood, himself included (25), do to get ahead, he keeps repeating, "Oh, God. I don't know what to do" (78) and "I'm *lost*" (79). Bobby's mind is made up when Karen says, "Bob, we have a meeting," meaning they will both be going to Ross to pitch the *Bridge* project. Charlie says, "I rest my case" (79), and Bob sends Karen out of the room. Karen's unpardonable offense is not prostituting herself in order to get ahead in the film business. After all, the men take pride in identifying themselves as "old whores." It is her presumption and her attempting to usurp Bobby's power that does her in. This is something that Charlie, who knows that "my job *is* kissing [Bob's] ass" (31), would never do, and in the end he is still in the game, at Bob's side, despite the fact that Bob has completely betrayed his loyalty when he decided to scrap his movie in favor of Karen's.

Karen's role has been the subject of controversy since the play's 1988 Broadway premiere, when the role got a disproportionate share of attention because it was played by pop icon Madonna. Most of the first night reviews were focused not on the play but on the question of whether or not Madonna could act. A few reviewers evoked Eve Harrington from the film *All about Eve,* suggesting that Karen is not so innocent as she seems. Most, however, like Mel Gussow, thought that in the purest sense, she is an ingenue—unknowing in Hollywood—not "a crafty Eve Harrington plotting her way to stardom or studio chiefdom."[39] In the more scholarly criticism since then, the disagreement persists.[40]

It is true that Madonna's portrayal in the original production presented Karen in an ambiguous light. As Jack Kroll suggested, Karen could be leading Bob onto the paths of spiritual redemption, or she could be "a more consummate con artist than the two aces themselves." Madonna, he wrote, turned her confrontation with Bobby "into a double seduction that scrambles all the moral angles. Who better than Madonna—Virgin, Material Girl—to give embodiment to the conundrum at the heart of David Mamet's scathingly comic play?"[41] To insist on Karen's naive innocence, or to suggest that her motives are not important, is to rob Karen of her agency and the play of a good deal of its complexity. To an audience aware of *Glengarry Glen Ross,* Mamet gives plenty of signals to suggest that Karen is conning Bobby from the beginning, in much the same way that Richard Roma cons James Lingk.

At the beginning of the play, Mamet's dialogue indicates that Bobby is uneasy with his new job and the power it brings, being somewhat fearful of his new responsibility for making decisions. His opening line is "When the gods would make us mad, they answer our prayers [. . .] I'm in the midst of the wilderness" (3). Although it is meant to be humorous, this statement betrays an underlying anxiety that is also suggested in the complaint that his new job is "one thing: the capacity to make decisions [. . .] decide, decide, decide" (24). When Charlie Fox arrives with the Doug Brown option, it is a lifesaver for Bobby, a true "no-brainer," a decision that he will not have to make. Karen, however, discovers his fear and plays on it, as she works her scheme to use *The Bridge* as her way into the movie business.

If Karen is truly naive about the movie business, her observation of the interaction between Charlie and Bob in act 1 tells her all she needs to know in order to get to work on Bob. The riff on being "old whores" (25–26) establishes the idea that prostituting oneself is the daily routine in Hollywood. Bob tells Charlie that, now that he is going to be a producer, he had better get ready for all the people who will plot against him to get his job, which is also business as usual. Revealing the weakness that would become the vehicle for Karen's own con, Gould describes Hollywood as a "sinkhole of slime and depravity" (28) and refers to "all that garbage that we put up with" (29), betraying his own dissatisfaction with the way he has to make his living there. Establishing the way Karen will need to operate in the movie business, the importance of the meeting with Ross is made clear, and Fox tells her that only when you have a "relationship" with someone in power, "then, you can do something" (30).

When Bob sets out to con Karen into sleeping with him, he starts by asking her, "you want a *thrill* in your life? [. . .] to *make* something, to *do* something, to be a *part* of something. Money, art, a chance to Play at the Big Table" (40). Karen answers yes, and she begins a gambit of her own, asking Bob whether the Doug Brown movie is "a good film" (40), a question that is meaningless to Bob, who responds, "well, it's a commodity" (41). Making clear that he is a businessman, not an artist, he says defensively, "some people are elected, try to change the world, this job is not that job," and he goes on about the pressures of a job in which someone is always trying to promote you (41). Under questioning from Karen, he admits, "this job corrupts you" (43). The uneasiness with the job's amorality that underlies his humor gives Karen the opening she needs. Like Ricky Roma's honing in on Lingk's fear of his wife, Karen pursues Bobby's sense of guilt and moral vacuity. She says that she would like the decision-making part of his job because "I would think that if you could keep your values straight, and you had *principles* to *refer* to, then . . ." (44). Bob admits that "if you don't have *principles*, whatever they are . . . then each day is hell, you haven't got a compass" (44–45).

Karen's pitch to Bob for the radiation film is centered on what she senses is most troubling to him, his fear of doing anything that will not obviously enhance the studio's bottom line. In her opening gambit, she tells Bob that *The Bridge* places the answer to the misery and the problems of the protagonist in one thing, the courage to face the fear of death. She says she felt empowered by the book, and that Bob too need not feel frightened if he embraces the book's message of change. She tells him that courage will put him at peace and bring love as well. Bob uses this opening to serve what he thinks is his own con of Karen, saying that he feels they have make a connection and that he wants to help her by giving her a job, but she derails his advance when she says she wants to work on the radiation film. When he tells her that it simply will not make a good movie and will not "Get The Asses In The Seats" (53), she counters with a warning not to reject the film because it is "too good" and says the people would come to see it because it is about what "we feel," that is, that everyone is frightened and everything is breaking down (54). She insists that the film will change everyone as it has changed her.

When Bob does not fall for this line, insisting that they are in business to *"make the thing everyone made last year. Make that image people want to see"* (56), Karen changes her strategy by confessing that she knew Bob wanted to sleep with her when he asked her to his house and saying she came because she too is weak and "we all need companionship" (58). After telling him they should not be afraid of needing each other, Karen manages to combine all her insight into Bobby's needs and weaknesses in a speech that rivals Roma's pitch to Lingk: "We prayed for a sign. A temporary girl. You asked read the book. I read the book. Do you know what it says? It says that you were put here to make stories people need to see. To make them less afraid. It says in *spite* of our transgressions—that we could do something. Which would bring us alive. So that we needn't feel ashamed. (*Pause.*) We needn't feel frightened. The wild animal dies with pride. He didn't make the world. God made the world. You say that you prayed to be pure. What if your prayers were answered? You asked me to come. Here I am" (59–60).

In act 3 it is clear that Karen's pitch has been successful, as they have spent the night together, and Bob is planning to do the radiation film instead of the Doug Brown picture, but then Karen comes up against Charlie and the real "principles" of the movie business. It is clear from Bob's language in talking about the film that Karen has put words in his mouth as well as ideas in his head. The summary he gives of the film is clearly the line that Karen has given him: "We are frightened . . . (*Pause.*) Because the World is Ending. Uh . . . (*Pause.*) A man gives up everything . . . wait. (*Pause.*) A man, to find happiness" (73).

Charlie presents Bob with the facts of the case as he sees them: "This broad *just took you down*" (72), and she is "A Tight Pussy wrapped around

Ambition" (78). He reminds Bob that in Hollywood the road to power for men is through work, but for women it is through sex. Countering Bob's weakness in believing that Karen likes him, Charlie reminds him, "you're nothing to her but what you can *do* for her" (72). When Karen admits that this is the case, her con fails. The naive and innocent temp who wants to help Bob make a film that will do good has been unmasked as an ambitious woman who wants the same thing Charlie wants, a producing credit on Bob's next film. She is no more a whore than Charlie is, but unlike Charlie she pretended to be something else. Although his motives are hardly pure, in taking the Doug Brown film to Bobby to ensure that he would receive his protection and a producing credit, Charlie has remained loyal to Bobby. Karen shows that she truly is innocent and naive in one way, in thinking that she can tell the truth about her motives for behaving as everyone in the business behaves.

Karen's con game having failed, she is banished from the office at the end, which restores the balance of power, as Charlie forgives Bob, saying, "I know what you wanted, Bob. You wanted to do good," and Bob replies, "I wanted to do Good . . . But I became foolish" (81). Bobby's newfound morality not only threatens the studio's bottom line and his career, it also subverts the only previous value he has articulated, Charlie's loyalty. With Bob back in the Hollywood mindset and Charlie back to "kissing his ass," they set off to make their movie with "Fox and Gould" above the title. The buddy film of Bobby and Charlie is thus restored along with the buddy film of Doug Brown and the "Flavor of the Month" (11), an apt comment on its durability. Bob would seem to have escaped being conned by Karen, whose basic honesty makes her an ineffective con artist in the end. But the encounter with Karen does suggest to Bob that there is a way out of the big con for which Hollywood makes such an effective synecdoche. Through Karen he glimpses the possibility that there are ethical principles: there is morality; there is authentic human connection. The weakness of this possibility in his world is a measure of the irony of Mamet's comedy. This is a world in which it is all but impossible to escape the reach of the big con.

All the victims of confidence games in Mamet's plays share a common trait that makes them vulnerable to con artists, big and small—a driving desire that they are unable to resist. Charles Lang must get his water engine made, regardless of the cost or the consequences. Miss A needs the psychological permission to contest her mother's will and perhaps to take revenge for her mother's rejection of her in favor of her stepfather. Aaronow seeks revenge on his bosses, an escape from his hated job, and a little money. James Lingk seeks escape from his sexual guilt and an opportunity to assert himself over his domineering wife along with the freedom and adventure that Roma's land deal promises. Karen, Bobby, and Charlie are all self-confessed whores who will sell themselves or anyone else out in a minute to get ahead in the movie business, but Bobby's weakness is that he desires some authentic feeling of worth in his life as well.

Constantly lurking in the background is the sense, made most palpable in *The Water Engine,* that the big con governs all, the game is fixed from the outset, and a sucker will never get an even break. In a world that is defined by the big con of the American Dream, it is desire itself that makes the characters vulnerable to a superior con artist whose major talent is the ruthless, emotionless exploitation of the weakness of others. Mamet's con artists exercise this talent to varying degrees, from the nearly humanitarian restraint of *The Shawl's* John to the winner-take-all play of a Ricky Roma or a Dave Moss. In showing us a spectrum of behavior within these given circumstances, Mamet suggests the possibility of exercising free will to make choices that result in personal satisfaction or fulfillment—material, psychological, emotional, even moral. But everything is personal. There are no universal values in this world, just a zero-sum game of winners and losers.

CHAPTER 7

Degeneration and Descent

Two of the plays Mamet lists among his tragedies, *American Buffalo* and *Oleanna,* portray a world of defeated possibility, where the hope of true human communication and empathy is destroyed by inevitable tragedy. Mamet has said that *American Buffalo* is "really a tragedy about life in the family," closely tied to the iconic American tragedy *Death of a Salesman.*[1] Most simply it is a play about the corruption of love and friendship by the pursuit of money. *Oleanna* is about the failed ideal of community that forms the myth of U.S. academia, specifically the collaborative devotion to teaching and learning on the part of students and teachers as a part of a disinterested and pure pursuit of knowledge.

American Buffalo, 1977

The play that really launched Mamet's reputation in the theater was *American Buffalo.* In the mid-1970s, its air of gritty realism and its carefully crafted illusion of Chicago street argot had shock value for audiences and reviewers, who spoke of the young playwright as something truly new on the American theatrical landscape. It was this play that introduced the dialogue of "Mametspeak," which produces the illusion of ordinary speech through broken sentences, lines that do not respond directly to each other, stichomythic exchanges, the deft use of expletives, and the brilliant use of arresting vernacular expressions. Dialogue such as the following exchange between Don, the owner of a junk shop, and Teach, a small-time criminal, uses all these techniques to convey Don's wounded pride at a perceived insult by a customer who had bought a buffalo nickel and Teach's distracted response to him:

DON: And he tells me he's the guy was in here yesterday and bought the
   buffalo off me and do I maybe have some other articles of interest.
TEACH: Yeah.
DON: And so I tell him, "Not offhand." He says that could I get in touch
   with him, I get some in, so I say, "sure," he leaves his card, I'm s'posed
   to call him anything crops up.
TEACH: Uh-huh.
DON: He comes in here like I'm his fucking doorman.
TEACH: Mmmm.
DON: He takes me off my coin and will I call him if I find another one.
TEACH: Yeah.
DON: Doing me this favor by just coming in my shop.
TEACH: Yeah.
Pause.
Some people never change.[2]

Mamet was disturbed by the many references to his dialogue as realistic street
speech, and he made efforts to correct this impression in early interviews. He
told Matthew Roudané, "All realism means is that the language strikes a
responsive chord. The language in my plays is not realistic but poetic. The
words sometimes have a musical quality to them. It's language that is tailor-
made for the stage. People don't always talk the way my characters do in real
life, although they may use some of the same words."[3]

   In the background of *American Buffalo* was the Veblenian view of capitalism that also informs *The Water Engine, Edmond, Glengarry Glen Ross,*
and *Speed-the-Plow.* Mamet said that, "as much as we might not like to think
so, these people are us. And, as Thorstein Veblen says, the behavior on this
level, in the lumpenproletariat, the delinquent class, and the behavior on the
highest levels of society, in the most rarefied atmospheres of the board room
and the most rarefied atmospheres of the leisure class is exactly identical."
Both groups are in fact "the people who create nothing, the people who do
nothing, the people who have all sorts of myths at their disposal to justify
themselves and their predators—and they steal from us. They rob the country
spiritually, and they rob the country financially."[4] These delinquent street
characters use the same myths to justify their behavior as the most high-flying
venture capitalists—"The freedom," as Teach so memorably puts it, "of the
individual [. . .] To Embark on Any Fucking Course that he sees fit [. . .] In
order to secure his honest chance to make a profit" (72–73). For Don and
Teach, this course includes breaking into a man's house to steal his coin
collection, a more direct form of robbery than Mamet would ascribe to the
denizens of the boardroom.

Mamet has said that *American Buffalo* is about honor among thieves, of "what is an unassailable moral position and what isn't. What would cause a man to abdicate a moral position he'd espoused?" Donny Dubrow's moral position is "that one must conduct himself like a man, and there are no extenuating circumstances for supporting the betrayal of a friend." The play is about "the betrayal of the fellow, Bobby, who he's teaching these things to."[5] As Mamet has pointed out, the critique of capitalism and the fact that *American Buffalo* is "finally a play about a family constellation"[6] mark its affinity with *Death of a Salesman*. It is the conjunction of these things with Mamet's uncanny evocation of the milieu of the marginal urban economy and the loving respect with which he creates his dialogue that makes this play unique.

American Buffalo begins with Don, the nurturing member of the family constellation, teaching Bobby the difference between friendship and business. Business, he says, is "people taking *care* of themselves," but he tells Bobby he has to "keep clear who your friends are, and who treated you like what. Or else the rest is garbage, Bob [. . .] There's lotsa people on this street, Bob, they want this and they want that. Do anything to get it. You don't have *friends* this life" (7–8). Mamet has designated Teach as Don's antagonist in the play, and has said that Don is "tempted by the devil [Teach] into betraying all his principles."[7] When Teach, who has lost so heavily at poker the night before that he has to pawn his watch, hears that Don is planning to send Bobby in to steal a customer's coin collection, he sets about undermining Don's confidence in Bobby in order to get the job for himself. He places Don's loyalty to Bobby directly in conflict with "business": "All I mean, a guy can be too loyal, Don. Don't be dense on this. What are we saying here? Business [. . .] All that I'm saying, don't confuse business with pleasure" (34). Convinced by Teach that he cannot afford to take a chance on Bobby, Don betrays his loyalty to "this young fellow whom he loves," as Mamet calls him,[8] and tries to assuage his conscience by buying him off with the fifty dollars Bobby requests.

A series of negotiations then takes place between Don and Teach, who are also supposed to be friends, as Teach challenges Don's competence by exposing his ignorance about the value of the coins and Don retaliates by exposing Teach's lack of professionalism in not knowing how he is going to get into the victim's house to steal the coins. Mirroring his betrayal of Bobby, Don betrays Teach by insisting on bringing in Fletcher, a man he believes is "a standup guy," with "skill and talent and the balls to arrive at [his] own *conclusions*" (4), on the job, thereby insulting Teach's professionalism as well as cutting into his prospective profits. Although Teach says he is hurt by this, he gives in, recognizing that Don has the upper hand in the negotiation. Act 1 ends with a two-word commentary on all of this as Don says to himself, "Fuckin' *business*" (55).

In act 2, after convincing Don that Fletcher has been cheating at poker, Teach puts Bobby's arrival with a buffalo nickel, which he says he found, together with the failure of Fletcher to show up on time for the job and implies to Don that they have been double-crossed, that Fletcher and Bobby have already done the burglary. He also says they are in league with Ruthie and Grace, whom Teach has been inveighing against since the beginning of the play for a perceived insult to him as a friend. Teach insists, "I don't fuck with my friends, Don. I don't fuck with my business associates. I am a businessman, I am here to do business, I am here to face facts" (83).

Bobby's fateful arrival with the news that Fletcher has been mugged and is in the hospital sets off the inevitable consequences of the first act's betrayals. Rather than seeing this situation as an explanation for Fletcher's failure to arrive on time, both Teach and Don take it as evidence that he has betrayed them, and the fact that Bobby says he has learned this from Grace is further evidence of their conspiracy. Seeking to trap Bobby in what they perceive is his lie, Teach grills him about the name of the hospital. When Bobby says it is Masonic, which Don proves with a phone call to be false, Don and Teach assume he is lying. Mamet has inserted a twist of tragic irony in that it is Teach himself who planted the suggestion of the name Masonic in Bobby's head, when he said sarcastically, "Here Fletch is in Masonic Hospital with a needle in his arm, huh" (88), and Bobby merely repeats it, saying he doesn't know why—"I just thought of it" (91).

Everything turns on this false revelation when Teach and Don believe they have proven Bobby a liar. Insisting that "loyalty does not mean *shit* a situation like this" (93), Teach goes after Bobby, hitting him on the head with a "*nearby object*" (94) when he keeps insisting, "I don't know anything" (94). Don becomes complicit with the words, "you brought it on yourself" (94). When the true revelation comes with Ruthie's phone call telling them that Fletcher is in Columbus Hospital, which is verified by Don, he realizes, too late, the enormity of his betrayal of Bobby. He tells Teach simply, "It's done now [. . .] I'm saying this is over" (98). Teach retaliates by hitting Don where he lives, insisting, "you fucking *fake*. You fuck your friends. You *have* no friends. No *wonder* that you fuck this kid around [. . .] you seek your friends with *junkies*. You're a joke on the street, you and him" (100–101). This scene leads Don to finally repudiate Teach and what he stands for: "the stinking deals you come in here [. . .] You stiff this one, you stiff that one . . . you come in here, you stick this poison in me [. . .] you make a life of garbage" (101). Bob's confession that he lied to Don that morning and had not really spotted the proposed victim leads to Teach's Veblenian outburst, as he flails about, wrecking the shop with a *"dead-pig sticker"* crying:

The Whole Entire World
There Is No Law.
There Is No Right And Wrong.
The World Is Lies.
There Is No Friendship[. . .] .
We all live like the cavemen. (103)

It is Don who has to prove the counter to this worldview, which he does when he forgives Teach by telling him he is not mad at him and tells Bobby he is sorry, which Bobby echoes. At the play's end, pathos, love, contrition and forgiveness are the dominant emotions as Don prepares to take Bobby to the hospital. Don has tragically realized that he has betrayed his friend for "business," which is exactly what he was trying teach Bobby not to do at the beginning of the play. It may have been Teach who introduced these corrupt values into his life, but it is he who has acted on them, and he is guilty of betraying his love for Bobby. As Mamet has succinctly put it, Don undergoes "recognition in reversal—realizing that all this comes out of his vanity, that because he abdicated a moral position for one moment in favor of some momentary gain, he has let anarchy into his life and has come close to killing the thing he loves. And he realizes at the end of the play that he has made a huge mistake, that rather than his young ward needing lessons in being an excellent man, it is he himself who needs those lessons. That is what *American Buffalo* is about."[9]

Oleanna, 1992

Oleanna is an overtly dystopian play. In order to make this clear, Mamet placed two epigraphs in the published version. One explains the play's title, which had proven confusing to audiences and reviewers of the earliest production by the Back Bay Theater Company in Boston. The epigraph is from a folk song that Mamet sang at YMCA camp:

Oh, to be in *Oleanna,*
That's where I would rather be.
Than be bound in Norway
And drag the chains of slavery.[10]

These lines describe a failed utopian community that was founded by the Norwegian musician Ole Bull and his wife, Anna, thus the name, Oleanna. The community failed because the farmland that was to support it proved rocky and infertile. The other epigraph, from Samuel Butler's *The Way of All Flesh*, describes the happy state of mind sustained by children who grew up in the poisonous air of the back alleys of nineteenth-century London, who "sing and play as though they were on a moor in Scotland." The chilling implication of this, Butler suggested, is that "the absence of a genial mental atmosphere is not commonly recognized by children who have never known it." Even if children are unhappy, "very unhappy—it is astonishing how easily they can be prevented from finding it out, or at any rate from attributing it to any other cause than their own sinfulness" (epigraph).

The application of these epigraphs to *Oleanna* is straightforward. The play's milieu is an American university, and in one sense the play is about the failed ideal of academia, the dream of an intellectual community in which knowledge is imparted from teacher to student in a generous, disinterested, and humane way for the good of all. Students should grow and thrive intellectually as a result of their teachers' efforts, and professors should feel pleasure and satisfaction in passing on the culture of learning to the next generation. In the face of this ideal, the play presents two self-absorbed people who feel fundamentally oppressed by the academic power structure as it inhibits their efforts to thrive in the world outside academia, while at the same time they exploit that power structure as much as they can to achieve their own ends.

Like many other Mamet plays, *Oleanna* is also about power and its relationship to language. In this case, as is indicated by the emphasis of the concept of a "term of art" at the beginning of the play, power is manifested by membership in certain privileged linguistic communities characterized by the use of a specialized language or jargon—the real estate business, academia, the feminist movement, and the legal system. The situation is that John, an assistant professor in his forties who is in the middle of the process by which he hopes to be granted tenure, is also in the process of buying a house, with his expectations based on tenure's promise of a secure income. Carol, a student who confesses herself bewildered by his class on education and unable to understand his book or the concepts and precepts in his class, comes to him, ostensibly for help.

In act 1 their first encounter is constantly interrupted by phone calls from John's wife about a possible problem with the easement for the house, a concept that he worries might be a term of art with implications he does not understand. Inextricably connected with this is his intense anxiety about the tenure process, exhibited in his urge "to *vomit*, to, to, to puke my *badness* on the table, to show them: 'I'm no good. Why would you pick *me*?'" (23). At the end of the act, when he is told that the phone calls have been a ruse to get him to a surprise party in the new house celebrating his tenure, he says, "there are those who would say it's a form of aggression" (41). For her part what Carol wants is for John to initiate her into the mystifying language of academia so that she can get good grades, earn a degree, and, as she says, "get on in the world" (12). She finds her inability to understand "the *language*, the 'things' that you say" (6) immensely frustrating. As Lenke Némath has pointed out, an analysis of the "adjacency pairs" of their dialogue shows that neither character has any interest in what the other is trying to communicate.[11]

Essentially, in the first act, John and Carol carry on parallel monologues, with each expressing his or her private anxieties, anxieties that come about because their personal ambitions are being thwarted by the entity that holds power over them in the context of the academic system—John, as Carol's professor, and "The Bad Tenure Committee," as the body that is deciding on the future of John's job, his career, and his family. Carol perceives herself as powerless within the academic structure, and she sees mastery of John's incomprehensible language as the key that will unlock the doors to success in the world that are now closed against her. John at first asserts his power over Carol through his use of the very language she says she cannot understand, and then, increasingly anxious about the real estate deal, which is tied up with his anxieties about tenure, he projects his own experience onto her, assuming the insecurity and self-doubts of his youth are identical to hers. Both are too absorbed in their own anxieties to listen to what the other is saying.

In act 2 there has been a shift in power, as we learn that Carol has gotten access to a new linguistic community, her feminist "Group," which has given her the language to describe John's words and actions in a way that puts him in danger with the Tenure Committee. John's opening monologue, laced with words like "gratuitously," "heterodoxy," and "paradigm," is calculated to overwhelm Carol, who in the first act needed explanations of "hazing" and "index." This time it does not work, however, for Carol, having found her own linguistic power base, is no longer awed by his. When she asks what "paradigm" means and he explains that it is a model, she says, "then why can't you use that word?" (45). John is confronted with Carol's complaint to the Tenure Committee, which accuses him of being elitist and of wasting time in "nonprescribed, in self-aggrandizing and theatrical *diversions* from the prescribed *text*" and that these offenses "have taken both sexist and pornographic forms" (47). This is clearly not Carol's language, but that of the group, which has empowered her linguistically to turn her discomfort at John's using an illustration contrasting the copulation practices of the rich and the poor into a charge that can lead to his losing his job. She defines this example as "*vile* and *classist,* and *manipulative* and *pornographic,*" saying "What gives you the *right*. Yes. To speak to a woman in your private" (51).

John's self-serving attempt to reorder the terms of the exchange by appealing to Carol to "agree that we are both human" (53) fails when he unintentionally reveals to her through a phone conversation that he is only interested in "dealing with the complaint" (55). Having failed at getting power over her linguistically, at the end of the act he is reduced to restraining her physically to try to get her to listen to him. This is his undoing, as it is Carol's language that defines his action. She responds by shouting "LET ME GO. LET ME GO. WOULD SOMEBODY *HELP* ME?" (57). In the third act, we learn that Carol and her group are in the process of pursuing criminal charges against John because "you 'pressed' your body into me," which, "under the statue. I am told. It was battery [. . .] And attempted rape" (78).

Having been empowered by the language of the legal system as well as her feminist Group, Carol now wields power over John. She tells him she will speak to the Tenure Committee if he supports her group's demand to ban a list of books, including his own, from "inclusion as a representative example of the university" (75). He takes a firm stand against this, insisting that "you're *dangerous,* you're *wrong* and it's my *job* . . . to say no to you" (76). When another phone call informs him about the possible criminal charges, he tells Carol to leave. But another turn is precipitated by Carol's eavesdropping. Listening to his phone conversation with his wife, she says, "don't call your wife baby" (79), assuming her authority to exert control over his most private linguistic community, his family. This command unleashes John's ultimate fury, as he is stripped of linguistic power and reduced to exerting the brute strength he has over her. He grabs her and beats her, spewing misogynistic invective: "you vicious little bitch [. . .] You little *cunt*" (79).

The relationship between teacher and student has thus been reduced to the raw exercise of power, which also reflects the ultimate power relation between men and women. Mamet has remarked notoriously in "True Stories of Bitches" that the ultimate response a man feels in an argument with his wife is "of course, physical violence": "if I get pushed just one little step further, why I might, I might just _____ (FILL IN THE BLANK) because she seems to have forgotten that I'M STRONGER THAN HER."[12] *Oleanna* is a case of a man stepping over that line. It ends ambiguously, with John lowering the chair he holds over Carol and sitting down at his desk. He looks at her and says, "well," and she looks at him, saying "Yes. That's right" and then looks away and says to herself, "yes. That's right" (80). There is a debate about the meaning of the ending, and of course it is entirely dependent on the interpretation a given director chooses to take in production.[13]

Most reviewers saw Mamet's original production as slanted in favor of John's position, although Mamet has insisted that "a lot of people thought the opposite."[14] In fact Mamet's interpretation was rather opaque. The ending of the production had Carol (Rebecca Pidgeon) crawling slowly out from under a bench where she ended up after the beating, while John (William H. Macy) sat at the desk at stage left.[15] He stared at her, and she looked straight out at the audience and then down as she said her line flatly, almost without intonation. This was an extension of Pidgeon's interpretation of the character under Mamet's direction, as she played Carol with a lack of facial expression, or with a flattened affect, a rather rigid body, and a flat, toneless voice, often blurting her lines. In the film version, also directed by Mamet, the look of bewilderment and then utter grief that crosses William H. Macy's face in close-up conveys his understanding of the implications of the brutality to which he has been reduced. What Carol means to affirm is more ambiguous. Thomas Goggans has developed an intriguing interpretation based on the analysis of the language in act 1, "a pastiche of phrases and clichés associated with the secrecy and psychological manipulation of incestuous abuse."[16] He suggests that Carol exhibits the signs of having been a victim of sexual abuse as a child, which would cause her to see herself as "bad" and worthy of punishment. This offers a credible explanation for Carol's statement, left hanging, that she has been "bad" all her life (38). Although Mamet has resisted the impetus to create "backstory" for his characters, this is a possibility that is suggested by the language itself. In his production Carol resisted any physical contact, breaking away brusquely from John when he puts his hand on her shoulder to comfort her, a cue that he of course missed, which was part of his undoing.

Another suggestion that is embedded in the language is that the more profound condition behind the lack of communication between John and Carol is a complete lack of empathy. While John has learned to make use of the vaguely humanistic language of education, his interaction with Carol reveals that he is incapable of actually listening to her, of entering imaginatively into her thoughts and feelings and responding to them. He uses language only to express his own thoughts and feelings, to lecture pedantically at length on a topic without any sensitivity to his listener's understanding or interest, or in a purely instrumental way, to manipulate his listener in order to achieve his desired result. Interestingly these are characteristics of Asperger's disorder, a condition that was first described in 1944 but that has only recently been added to the *Diagnostic and Statistical Manual of Mental Disorders*. In *Bambi vs. Godzilla,* David Mamet has written a tantalizing piece, "Jews in Show Business," in which he suggests that "Asperger's syndrome helped make the movies." Mamet's theory is that, since Asperger's has "its highest prevalence among Ashkenazi Jews and their descendants" and Ashkenazi Jews are also "the bulk of America's movie directors and studio heads,"[17] it is reasonable to assume that Asperger's is prevalent among them as well. In his essay Mamet hinted that Asperger's may well be present in his own family, for all four of his Ashkenazi grandparents had come from the same area around Warsaw as "the men who made the movies—Goldwyn, Mayer, Schenck, Laemmle, Fox" (20).

Mamet listed the more productive characteristics of Asperger's as typical of film directors: "early precocity, a great ability to maintain masses of information [. . .] high intelligence [. . .] A preternatural ability to concentrate on the minutiae of the task at hand," along with traits that are generally considered negative but which can be quite helpful to the film director, such as "a lack of ability to mix with groups in age-appropriate ways" and "ignorance of or indifference to social norms" (19). His description of the disorder is slanted toward the positive, but it suggests an acquaintance with people who have the condition. The *Psychiatric Dictionary* describes Asperger's syndrome as follows: "a hypertrophy of intellect at the expense of feeling and manifested as one or more of the following: lack of sensitivity, empathy, intuition, and normal human understanding; inappropriate one-sided social interaction; pedantic speech, which is more a proclamation than a conversation; inability to make friends; clumsiness and poor motor coordination."[18]

This is a most accurate description of John, who talks constantly about human understanding but is unable to break out of his own solipsistic self-absorption to perceive Carol, let alone understand her. Even when he is trying to be sympathetic to what she is going through, he can see her only as a younger version of himself, so he projects his own remembered fears and frustrations onto her. He thinks she will identify with and be encouraged by his admission that he hated school and teachers and bosses when he was young and with his dismissal of academic tests as *"garbage"* and *"a joke"* (23) and his contempt for the members of the Tenure Committee. On the issue of authority, however, Carol is the polar opposite of John. She does not want to overthrow the hierarchy of power; she wants access to it. She is offended by his hypocrisy in mocking the academic system at the same time that he is trying to ensure his future by obtaining tenure within it.

The inevitable course of tragic misunderstanding in this play is ensured by the fact that Carol is no more capable of empathy than John is. Mamet has hinted that Carol shares Asperger's traits with John at the beginning of the play, when she exhibits her "indifference to or ignorance of social norms" in her first encounter with John. She not only eavesdrops on his conversation with his wife, she bluntly asks him after he hangs up, "what is a 'term of art'" (2), referring to one of its details. In Mamet's production Pidgeon blurted this out in an almost childlike way. In the course of the play, when John replies with irritation, she responds in a way that suggests she has no understanding of appropriate behavior in this situation: "Did I . . . did I . . . did I say something wr . . ." (3). In the interchange that follows, she bluntly contradicts John five times, showing a marked insensitivity to the fact that her responses in this encounter are not constructive. She is presumably there, after all, to get help from John, or at least to get him to change her grade.

Later in act 1, Carol interrupts John's personal confession about his anxieties to ask about her grade, showing that she has no appreciation for the delicacy of the topic and no sense of his emotional intensity, and then she asks, "Is that bad [. . .] Is it bad that I asked you that? [. . .] Did I upset you?" (24–25). Carol's difficulty with the social context, despite the fact that, as John says, she is "an incredibly bright girl" (7), erupts in her confession that she has no understanding of how to interact with other people in the context of academia: "I'm *smiling* in class, I'm *smiling*, the whole time. What are you *talking* about? What is everyone *talking* about? I don't *understand*. I don't know what it *means*. I don't know what it means to *be* here . . . you tell me I'm intelligent, and then you tell me I should not be *here*, what do you *want* with me? What does it *mean*? Who should I *listen* to?" (36).

In act 3, when John is basically pleading with her not to get him fired, Carol shows a marked insensitivity to his reminders that his wife and child are dependent on his income. When John finally asks her twice, "Don't you have feelings?" (65), she evades this question, referring abstractly to her responsibility to "this institution. To the *students*. To my *group*" (65). The emotional affect that Carol shows is of course up to the director and the actor in a particular production. In Mamet's production Rebecca Pidgeon played this scene without obvious emotion, but with a kind of obsessive intensity, as Carol is intent on revealing the truth to John, a truth that she sees as absolute, that "You're wrong. I'm not wrong. You're wrong" (68). Her delivery of the lines, which read as somewhat strange and stilted on the page, made them seem natural to Carol, whose blurted language matches her lack of affect. In the production Carol came across as absolutely sincere in her desire to bring the truth to John, without another agenda except the tragic one of seeking the understanding that is impossible between them. In Mamet's film Debra Eisenstadt projects a persona that is detached and devoid of empathy, but more calculating. The film suggests that her actions against John are motivated more by the agenda of her group than her own obsession with stating the truth as she sees it.

Given these two people and their constitutional lack of empathy, it is inevitable that their encounter will lead to misunderstanding. That it leads to disaster is the tragedy of the play. And as the play's protagonist, it is John who precipitates that disaster. As Mamet has said, "it's structured as a tragedy. The professor is the main character. He undergoes absolute reversal of situation, absolute recognition at the last moment of the play. He realizes that perhaps he is the cause of the plague on Thebes."[19] In this tragic world that Mamet has set up, reflective of classical Greek tragedy, it is not uncontrollable forces like fate or biology that count, but actions. As Carol ruthlessly informs John: "What has *led* you to this place? Not your sex. Not your race. Not your class. YOUR OWN ACTIONS" (64).

Bobby Gould in Hell 1989, and *Faustus,* 2004

As Toby Zinman has suggested, the descent into hell motif is at the core of several Mamet plays.[20] *Bobby Gould in Hell* and *Faustus* consider the possibility of a hellish eternity as the just deserts of his protagonists. *Bobby Gould* is a humorous fantasy about a contemporary Everyman, and *Faustus* is a modern version of the Faust legend, but they share a sense of sin and evil that helps to define Mamet's moral viewpoint. Bobby has been condemned to hell for having "caused pain"[21] to others, and he is being kept there because, thinking he is no worse than the average, he refuses to admit that he is a bad man. Bobby's major sin turns out to be that he has broken a woman's heart. He is given the chance to go back to Earth and right the wrongs he has done, "alleviate 'sorrow,' 'cruelty'" (41), but he almost damns his soul forever by asking what he gets if he does not choose to do this. He quickly realizes what he has done, saying "I don't know why I acted the way I did. But I'm so sorry" (44). With that he is pardoned and allowed to go home, telling his Interrogator that he has changed, that his experience in hell has brought him to see that "real humanity can come only through suffering, That none of us is perfect. But all of us are human" (45).

While Mamet's Faustus has the traditional traits of ambition and overweening pride, his play puts the original story of the man who sells his soul to the devil in the context of the family. This Faustus sins by ignoring the cries of his sick child while he is intent on learning the secret of a magician's trick. The constant calls to come to the child in act 1 are interrupted by the temptation of the devil in the form of the Magus, who promises to reveal secrets to him. Faustus finally damns his soul by swearing on the lives of his wife and son in order to get the Magus to reveal what he says is a flaw in Faustus's magnum opus, just completed. The Magus reveals a simple trick and says that his wife and child are dead. In the second act Faustus is in hell, where a vision of his wife reveals his sin to be that he "strove for fame. For the delusion of popular love," to which he sacrificed his son, an "unnatural vicious father" (92). In both of these plays, the significant moral relation is not between human being and God but between persons. The sins are betrayal, cruelty, failure to love, disloyalty, selfishness, and self-absorption. The possibility for redemption comes from recognizing these elements in oneself and trying to make up for them.

In plays such as *The Water Engine, Edmond,* and *Glengarry Glen Ross,* Mamet used the symbolic motif of a hell on earth, created by the inhumanity of a society that has self-interest as its moving principle and "raping and pillage" as its economic system, as a means of examining the existential condition of the contemporary American male. The motif of the confidence game informs these plays as well, contributing to the sense that other human beings are not only completely self-interested, but tricky and dangerous, and our perception of reality itself cannot be trusted.

Edmond, 1982

Like *The Water Engine, Edmond* incorporates confidence games that are used as both a dramaturgical element and a thematic vehicle for conveying Mamet's philosophical and political concerns. Since its premiere many critics have noted that *Edmond* has a great deal in common with Georg Büchner's *Woyzeck,* an influence Mamet has acknowledged, and the German expressionist "Stationen" plays, the best-known of which is Georg Kaiser's *From Morn to Midnight* (1922). As Jon Tuttle has pointed out, Kaiser's play provides the model of the little man, a Cashier, who literally breaks out of his cage and sets out to find "what's for sale" in the world. The Cashier's speech, as he testifies at a Salvation Hall, articulates much of Mamet's own early thinking about the capitalistic economic system: "You can buy nothing worth having [. . .] You get less than you pay, every time. The more you spend, the less the goods are worth. The money corrupts them: the money veils the truth. Money's the meanest of the paltry swindles in this world!"[22] In the context of the 1982 production of *Edmond* at the Provincetown Playhouse in Greenwich Village, Mamet sounded a familiar Veblenian note to an interviewer: "The American Dream has gone bad [. . .] It was basically raping and pillage." Because we "are finally reaching a point where there is nothing left to exploit," he said, "the dream has nowhere to go so it has to start turning in on itself [. . .] The myth of the so-called American Dream doesn't work anymore and as a result the people it has sustained, the white males, are going nuts. What they wish for is peace but they are overcome by fear. They must insure their position; they must get ahead; they must make a billion dollars; they must have younger and skinner women; all this is driving them insane."[23]

Ultimately, Mamet suggested, *Edmond* is about empathy. "It is impossible to have spiritual empathy if you don't have spirit. That is what is lacking [. . .] That is what each person has to discover in himself. How much empathy is there in a society that is founded on the belief and fear that if I go up, you go down?"[24] He has also said that Theodore Dreiser's *An American Tragedy* had a great influence on his conception of the play: "It's always struck me what a great achievement it would be if I could one day write a scene to make people understand why somebody killed."[25]

In *Edmond,* Edmond Burke (an allusion to the conservative British historian) leaves his wife, who, he says, does not interest him sexually or spiritually, and he sets out on a nightmarish journey through New York's seedy all-night sex districts to see what his money will buy. There are two catalysts for his figurative descent into hell. The Fortune-Teller tells him that life is predetermined, with one's destiny manifested by "signs" of diet, genes, or stars, and that Edmond is special and not where he belongs. The notion of determinism probably derives from Dreiser. The other catalyst is a man Edmond meets in a bar. He tells him he wishes he were a "nigger" because they seem to have it easy, without the "pressure" that whites have, and he tells Edmond he needs to escape the pressure through the means that are available to him: "*Pussy . . . Power . . . Money . . .* uh *. . . adventure* [. . .] self-*destruction* [. . .] *religion* [. . .] *release,* uh, ratification."[26] Agreeing with the man that what he needs is to "get laid" because he does not "feel like a man" (228), Edmond sets out in search of sex.

The defining characteristic of Edmond's quest for sexual contact is that every attempt is a monetary exchange in which he wants to pay only what the act is worth to him, and in every exchange he is cheated or conned out of more money than he thinks he should pay. In his first encounter, he naively tells a B-Girl that "I'm putting myself at your *mercy* [. . .] I don't want to be taken advantage of" (230). When she tries to sell him overpriced drinks that he knows are tea, he says, "I came here to be *straight* with you, why do we have to go *through* this?" (232), and he is ejected from the bar. In a peep show, he obsesses about his change and then leaves when he finds out the plexiglass barrier between him and the performer will not come down. "You're only cheating your*self,*" she says (235). Edmond's standards for civilized behavior are assaulted by his constant frustration as he descends further and further down the ladder of middle-class respectability. In a massage parlor he keeps insisting that the price the prostitute wants for sex is "too much, on top of the sixty-eight at the door" (242). When she demands payment in cash instead of the credit card that he was told would be accepted, he confusedly thanks her as she sends him off to cash a check in a restaurant.

Edmond's growing frustration at these failed monetary exchanges explodes when he is conned by a three-card-monte scam on the street. For the first time, he fights back, demanding to see the cards, but the dealer and his shill beat him up and take his wallet. The callous treatment by a hotel night clerk who will not tell him whether he needs a coin to call American Express on the pay phone brings out a greater explosion of anger, in which, as with the B-Girl, he pits human values against economic self-interest, evoking the Golden Rule: "Do you want to live in a *world* like that? I've been *hurt*? Are you *blind*? Would you appreciate it if I acted this way to *you*?" (249).

In a pawnshop Edmond fares better, according to his lights, as the pawnbroker is straight with him about the details of the transaction. When Edmond asks what his wedding ring is worth, the broker explains that he will give him only a quarter of the value, and Edmond agrees. In another transaction at the pawnshop, however, he is talked into buying "the best knife that money can buy" (254), although the broker neglects to tell him it is illegal, an omission which later gets him arrested. Making another attempt at human connection on the subway, he scares a woman when he tells her she is wearing a hat like his mother's. He grabs her, and, as she tries to get away, explodes "who the fuck do you think you *are*? . . . I'm *talking* to you . . . What am I? A *stone*?" (255). In his next transaction, with a pimp on the street, Edmond bargains down the price of oral sex to what he thinks is fair and asks, "Is that alright?" (258). When the pimp explains that he needs the money up front so he can be sure Edmond is not a cop, he actually apologizes for trying to withhold it until he sees the prostitute. But the pimp's attempt to rob him unleashes his rage again, and, screaming racial and sexual insults, he beats and kicks him, finally spitting on him. He walks away, saying "I hope you're *dead (Pause.)* Don't fuck with *me*, you *coon*" (261).

Elated from his victory over the pimp, Edmond exults to Glenna, who waits on him in a coffeehouse, about being "*alive*" (262), and they go back to her apartment and have sex. He tells the story of beating up the pimp, treating it as a moment of revelation and release about the racism he had been harboring during years of liberal guilt: "I DIDN'T FUCKING WANT TO UNDER-STAND . . . let *him* understand *me* . . . I wanted to KILL him. *(Pause.)* In that *moment* thirty years of prejudice came out of me [. . .] For the first *time*, I swear to God, for the first *time* I saw: THEY'RE PEOPLE, TOO" (265), this despite the fact that he had reduced the man to racist epithets, completely denying him any individual human identity. In this scene he does the same thing with gay men, saying that he hates them because "they suck cock. (*Pause.*) And that's the truest thing you'll ever hear" (266). At this point Edmond thinks he has learned the secret of how to live: "This world is a piece of shit. (*Pause.*) It is a shit house. (*Pause.*) . . . There is no law . . . there is no *history* . . . there is just *now* . . . and if there is a *god* he may love the weak, Glenna. (*Pause.*) But he respects the strong (*Pause.*) And if you are a *man* you should be feared" (266).

Glenna refuses to accede to Edmond's demand to "be what you *are*" (269) and "change your life with me" (270), and she becomes more and more afraid of him, finally saying that he is the devil and screaming for help. He stabs her with the knife from the pawnshop, saying "*now* look what you've bloody fucking done" (273). Questioned by a policeman after the woman from the subway recognizes him just as he is about to testify in a storefront church, he lies about his identity and is arrested when the cop finds the knife. As he is being interrogated about the woman on the subway, he says that what he did was the equivalent of kicking a dog: "I made a simple, harmless comment to her, she responded like a fucking bitch" (279). The interrogator, however, reveals that the police know about his murdering Glenna, and he ends up in jail.

When Edmond is put in with an African American cellmate, he reveals his state of mind, saying "when we *fear* things, I think that we *wish* for them" (284). He tells his cellmate that he thinks white people should be in prison "to be with black people [. . .] because we're *lonely*" (285). His cellmate offers him a cigarette, generally recognized as hard currency within the prison economy, and Edmond declines it, saying "not just now" (286). The man says, "I think you should just get on my body [. . .] now don't you want to do that?" (286). Given that Edmond's previous remarks could be taken as a sexual invitation and the man offers him a cigarette, an exchange that mirrors Edmond's transactions with the prostitutes, his supposition is not out of line. When Edmond refuses, he offers him a choice between the act and death, saying "Les' get this out the way" (287). The cellmate is not only fulfilling Edmond's suspicion that the fear, in his case homophobia and racism, "hides a wish" (284), the desire to have sex with this man, he is also establishing himself as "a man" according to the creed that Edmond laid down for Glenna. He is the stronger, the more powerful, the phallic, and therefore the male in the cell.

In the next scene Edmond tells the prison chaplain that he feels alone and empty and rejects the idea that God is the answer unless he can cause him to walk out of jail a free man and "cause a new *day*. In a perfect land full of *life*.

And *air*. Where people are *kind* to each other, and there's *work* to do. Where
we grow up in *love* and in security we're *wanted*" (289). Asked why he killed
the girl, he can only stammer over and over, "I . . . (*Pause.*) I . . . (*Pause.*) I
don't . . . *I*" (290). The final scene has been the source of a good deal of critical controversy. Edmond and his cellmate lie on their bunks discussing destiny, an exchange that becomes funny, as they consider the possibility of some
"whacked-out sucker" (294) in the Ozarks knowing the secrets of life and the
possibility of animals from outer space having been put on earth to watch
over us, but it ends rather poignantly as they consider whether there is a hell
and they are in it, or whether they will go somewhere when they die.

Although C. W. E. Bigsby dismissed this conversation as "swap[ping]
banalities,"[27] Dennis Carroll contended that the rhythms of the language suggest an authentic relationship "marked by genuine rapport [. . .] it overlaps but
moves in consonant rhythms. It is not an instance of a parallel monologue. The
men anticipate each other's thoughts, so that in spite of their differences they
are in tune with each other."[28] His reading is certainly accurate. The rhythms
and the sense of the dialogue suggest men who are deeply in tune with each
other, who respect each other's thoughts and are accustomed to listening:

PRISONER: Or maybe *we're* the animals . . .
EDMOND: . . . Maybe we are . . .
PRISONER: *You* know, how they, *they* are supreme on their . . .
EDMOND: . . . Yes.
PRISONER: On their *native* world . . .
EDMOND: But when you put them here.
PRISONER: *We* say they're only *dogs,* or *animals,* and *scorn* them . . .
EDMOND: . . . Yes. (296)

While the two men are clearly engaged with each other, their conversation
cannot be taken as serious intellectual engagement with the philosophical
issues they are grappling with. Richard Brucher has suggested that "Mamet
intends the talk to be superficial and disconcerting" and that the ending is
"parodic, a travesty of the sort of recognition we expect to experience in
moralities and tragedies."[29] But the questions they end with—whether there
is an afterlife and whether they are living through a hell on earth—are primal
and universal, and the cellmate's responses to Edmond, that he does not know
if they are in hell and that he hopes they will go somewhere when they die,
are authentic human responses. Mamet has said that *Edmond* is about "someone searching for the truth, for God, for release."[30] He seems none too sure
he has found this at the end of the play.

On the other hand, the relationship that Edmond has with his cellmate seems to offer some human connection that transcends the mercenary terms that permeate almost every human interaction in the play. Dennis Carroll notes that in Gregory Mosher's original production, the good-night kiss that ends the final conversation "was intense, with a searching look indicative of deep love and affection" (104), but each man ended the scene in his own bunk, an image of ultimate isolation. In the 2006 film, for which Mamet wrote the screenplay, the two men kiss affectionately, and then get into bed together, the cellmate putting his arm over Edmond as Edmond grins. There is, however, the fact that Edmond was forced into sex by this man. Bigsby suggested that in being forced to become the "wife" of his cellmate, Edmond simply experiences an inversion of his earlier sexual aggression against women.[31] Another critic has maintained that Edmond descends into "being a prisoner in bondage to a homosexual partner."[32] There is clearly an element of human communication and affection in this relationship, however, that takes it beyond bondage. To use Mamet's term, it is of a higher "spiritual" quality than the marriage bond between Edmond and his wife, which is not, as he tells her, one of those marriages where the wife would be inclined to stand by him, although he acknowledges that at times they wished that they could be "closer to each other" (283).

The key to the final line may be in Edmond's idea that "every fear hides a wish" (284). Mamet suggests that Edmond's homophobia and racism are the result of a lifetime of fear of the Other in black people and perhaps an element of homosexual panic. Edmond is quick to agree with Glenna that he hates "faggots" because "they suck cock" (266), and when the police interrogator asks him if he is gay, he retorts, "What business is that of yours?" (279) and denies it. In suggesting to his cellmate that every fear hides a wish and expressing his desire to "be with black people," however, he may be expressing unconscious or repressed homoerotic desire. Mamet has said that, at the end of the play, Edmond's "sexual identity, his social identity, his racial identity have been fractured and discarded"[33] and that "only at the end of the play, after having completely destroyed his personality, does he realize how incredibly destructive and hateful an attitude [his] is."[34]

Deprived of his freedom, his money, and his socially imposed but empowering identities of husband and white heterosexual male, Edmond has had to find another way of relating to his cellmate and to his very existence than he has previously. He is in jail; he may be in hell; but there are compensations. He has the thing he has been looking for throughout the play, a sexual relationship that includes honest, authentic human communication, a spiritual dimension, however banal, that the men share, and, most important, no element of monetary exchange. In the end, Mamet has said, because Edmond "winds up in a homosexual alliance with a black guy [. . .] because he resolves those basic dichotomies, I think it's a very, very hopeful play."[35]

CHAPTER 8

The Novels

In a 1994 television interview, Mamet explained why he had taken to writing fiction. "I always wanted to be a writer, and to me a writer was somebody who wrote novels. That's what a writer was, and anything else was, was not a writer, so I figured, well, hell with it, if you want to be one, why don't you try it."[1] The result of his effort has been three novels so far, each ambitious in its literary aims and all completely different in aesthetics and technique. Mamet referred to *The Village* (1994) as "a kind of laconic, stoic, Northern novel" with an epic form, in the sense that "each person has his, his own interest, and the people are, in this novel, held together by a theme [. . .] How does one live in a harsh climate?"[2] It is based on his experience of living part of each year in the tiny village of Cabot, Vermont, for twenty years before he wrote the novel. Its fragmented narrative, split among various citizens of the village, is written in a spare, minimalist realism. *The Old Religion* (1997) is based on a historical event, the 1914 case of Leo Max Frank, a Jewish businessman who was falsely accused of murdering one of the workers in the Atlanta textile factory he ran. A series of meditations in the mind of Frank, it is closer to a modernist experiment in narrative subjectivity than a typical historical novel. Although it is imbued with the spirit of postmodernism, *Wilson: A Consideration of the Sources* (2001) is sui generis, a postapocalyptic novel in which the apocalypse is the crash of the Internet, which was one of the catastrophes that many had feared with the arrival of the year 2000. In one sense the book is a 336-page joke on academic scholars who try to generalize about civilization from the odd fragments they focus on; in another it is an extended meditation on the decline of civilization and the impossibility of arriving at a viable sense of truth.

The Village, 1994

Mamet has said that he wrote *The Village* as a series of separate scenes, and the novel has a cinematic quality, as if each section were being focalized through a particular character's point of view. There are six major characters. Henry, still an outsider to the village despite his long residency, reflects Mamet's own relationship to Cabot and its residents. Although his profession is not identified, Henry may easily be a writer, as he has no fixed schedule and thinks deeply about the proper container for the pencils on his desk. Dick is the owner of the local hardware store, where the men gather, a store that is gradually sinking into foreclosure throughout the year of the book's narrative. Marty is a mechanic, a good father and husband, and a skilled woodsman and hunter. Lynn is an old farmer who has taken on the role of mentor to Henry, teaching him about hunting and the outdoors. Bill, the state trooper, goes through a series of police calls that include domestic violence and death. He is having an affair with Maris, the young beauty of the village, whose sexual promiscuity is the cause for a great deal of interest and concern among the villagers. While the novel conveys the transcendent beauty of the harsh northern landscape and the value of authentic community in the village, the common thread of the narrative is the disintegration that is taking place beneath the surface. Henry's marriage is falling apart; Dick and his wife are losing their store; Maris's risky behavior teeters on the verge of disaster; male-female relations in general seem to be descending into cyclic violence; nature, which is the source of great beauty for the characters, also provokes terror for Henry.

In the discrete sections of the novel, the identities of the focal characters are kept deliberately vague through the use of pronouns so that the reader is forced to become alert to discovering them through various cues, often several paragraphs into the section. As Bigsby has suggested, "the blurring of identities serves both to suggest their exemplary status and to imply that together these characters constitute the corporate identity which is the village, not so much a place as an experience, though one separately encountered and interpreted."[3] This withholding of identity is also part of the aesthetic design of the novel, which owes a good deal to Ernest Hemingway's iceberg theory, "that you could omit anything if you knew that you omitted and the omitted part would strengthen the story and make people feel something more than they understood."[4] As Mamet paraphrased it, "Hemingway said it once: 'To write the best story you can, take out all the good lines.'"[5] Although he has resisted direct comparisons, Mamet has acknowledged Hemingway's influence, comparing his effect on American writing to that of Marlon Brando on

American acting. Brando, he said, "revolutionized the American notion of what it meant to act" with his portrayal of Stanley Kowalski.[6]

Like Hemingway, Mamet omitted elements of the story while making the description of the landscape, the symbolic resonance of objects, and the detailed description of the characters' actions do the work of making readers feel more than they consciously understand. The novel begins from the point of view of Henry, who is ill. He thinks, if only "there were someone to bring me an aspirin or a glass of cooling water,"[7] which seems an odd thought, since his wife comes into the bedroom periodically to check on him. When she brings him soup, he cannot stand the smell and cannot eat it. This disgust at his wife's nurturing attempts extends to a general sense of rot. He consults the doctor about the possibility of having an infection in his nose: "Henry did not want to say he could smell it, but that is what he would have to say to tell him—'I can smell it. It smells like my body's rotting, or a wound, when it goes bad'" (15). This sense of rot is picked up in the most telling representation of Henry's feelings about his marriage, after he dreams that he has lost his children, leaving them on a streetcar in the rain. He hears the apples falling from a tree in the yard and thinks about the natural process of the apple's separation from the tree: "if the forces of nature are conjoined to *rot* it; and to rot it *first,* so that it *separates* from the tree, what intercession could there be? Who would want to suspend all natural laws, to cause the stem to adhere past the time when . . ." (122). As he thinks about the apple, the slamming screen door indicates the presence of his wife, and he thinks, "What can she want?," shutting her out of his consciousness, which provokes her outburst, "'Don't you *think,*' she said, her voice full and sure, 'that you might do me the *courtesy* of paying me polite *attention,*' she said, 'when I am *addressing* you?'" (124). As a whole the scene constitutes a representation of Henry's anxieties about quitting a marriage that is clearly over.

Another resonant image is that of the kestrel chicks that everyone in the village keeps shooing out of the road so they do not get run over. The men in Dick's store advance a number of theories to explain the chicks' being in the road, such as the attraction of salt and gravel. When Henry comes upon them, he sees one of the chicks perched on his dead sibling. Taking the romantic view—"if he is going to stay there, on his lost Mate, let me get it off the road, and into the woods" (107)—he looks around for a stick to help him move the carcass while he wonders if it is "some instinct of mutual aid" that causes the bird to stay with his mate. When he comes back, however, he finds that "the one was eating the corpse of the other" (107). Leaving the scene, he feels "marginally less deluded than the men in the Store" (108), who otherwise have a much better knowledge of the natural world than he does. Neither

Henry nor the narrator mentions Henry's marriage at this point, but the attentive reader does not need that mention to see the significance of the encounter for Henry.

Perhaps the most Hemingwayesque aspect of *The Village* is the depiction of Henry's use of carefully structured physical activity to evade his troubled state of mind. As Nick Adams follows his self-prescribed rules for hiking and fishing, Henry exercises his carefully acquired knowledge of North Country life when splitting wood, tracking deer, and building a fire. Hunting in the woods, he feels elated when he picks up the trail of a deer emerging from a stream: "He'd been on the deer's trail for two hours. He had lost it early on, then found it, and followed the tracks down to the stream. He'd cast upstream and down, as the books he'd read told him; first one bank and then the opposite, and had finally located this spot where the deer came out" (167). Making himself some tea in the woods, he thinks, "if I had any courage at all, I'd live out here; and to hell with it. I'd live out here" (169).

Henry's image of himself as competent in the woods is undermined by the superior woodsman Marty, who is truly at home there. When Marty tracks his deer, he simply goes to where they will be and sits still, as his grandfather had taught him, "for you had to be like it if you wanted to be part of it" (194). Marty sits from before dawn until after dark with his back against a tree, thinking about his family and the past, until "for longer periods, as the day went on, he thought about nothing, and missed nothing that went on before him and around him" (197). As the darkness closes in, Marty is rewarded by the appearance of four deer, and he carefully takes aim at the buck. Henry's appearance during Marty's vigil clearly marks the difference between the outsider and the man who is at home in the woods. Sitting by his tree, Marty hears the snapping of twigs and sees Henry "moving heavily down to the stream-bed [. . .] Henry moved over the stones in the stream, holding his rifle high, and sweeping the banks with his eyes. He swept his glance right over Marty, who knew he would not be observed, then moved on" (196).[8]

Unlike Marty, Henry never succeeds in killing a deer, and he courts disaster by getting lost in the woods, an image, and probably a result, of his emotional state over his marriage. In a narrative reminiscent of Jack London's "To Build a Fire," Henry is confident of his woodsman's skills as he begins to track a deer on cross-country skies, but he gets lost, lacks competence in using his compass, and finally loses his compass and a back-up as well as his hat, and, numbing his hands as he digs for the compass in the snow, risks frost-bite as well. As desperation and confusion from hypothermia set in, he runs frantically down a logging road, hoping it is the one that leads to the road to his house. On the verge of losing his wits, he comes out on the road, finding that he was within a few yards of it all the time. With his face burning with the cold and no feeling in his hands, he makes his way toward home, that is "his house, and the yellow light in the kitchen, and the shadow which was his wife" (210).[9]

The emotional states of Dick and Maris are characterized through similar indirection. The sense of what Dick risks losing in his store is invested in the old railroad stove that heats it in the winter. At the beginning of the novel, before his financial situation becomes a crisis, Dick looks at the fire and thinks of riches: "the *truth* of the matter is, I'm a warm son of a bitch in dry clothes in front of this very stove, smoking my pipe; and, as to what may happen tomorrow or this afternoon, that is not ours to know; and that's the god-damn truth" (57). In course of the narrative, his peace of mind is lost along with his very identity, which was invested in owning the store, for, as he fantasizes telling the bank's loan officer, "a *store,* you stupid fucking shit, is what the man who *is* the store has put into it" (163). In the end, however, it is the banker's view of the world that prevails, and Henry, deep in a meditation on the value of community, heads for the store and the group of men he expects to find there, but he is stopped short by a padlock on the door.

Maris's sexual abuse by her mother's boyfriend, whom she can not be induced to call her stepfather, is indicated not by any interaction between them, but by her detachment from the series of older men she has sex with in the course of the narrative and by her shockingly violent thoughts about him. "She thought the muscles in his shoulders were too well developed beneath the grey t-shirt, and she thought the shirt was rank with tired sweat from too many hours driving, and there was nothing attractive in the smell [. . .] 'I hate that shirt,' she thought, 'and the smell of it, as much as anyone has ever hated anything'" (13). She fantasizes about hitting him in the head with a crowbar and dragging him back into the woods, where she could chain him in an abandoned mineshaft until he screamed and whimpered, and about torturing him with a knife, until she gave him a choice, "put out your eyes or cut your *dick* off." "'You fucking cocksucker,' she thought [. . .] 'What are you *screaming* for?' she thought. 'Don't you *like* it . . . ?'" (139). Maris's physical loathing for his body and the details of her revenge fantasy are all suggestive of sexual abuse, as is the fact that she has no emotional connection either to her mother or to her sexual partners. Everyone in the village who is not sleeping with Maris seems to worry about the end she will reach. Seeing an out-of-state car parked with the engine running, Rose, the postmistress, knows it is Maris "in there with some man. 'One day,' she thought, 'they're going to find her dead in the woods'" (83).

They do not find Maris dead in the woods. Instead she just vanishes, leaving behind the villagers' theories. Bill, the trooper, who has been one of her sex partners, tells Lynn, the old farmer, that "Sm'b'y killed her, dragged her off . . . I don't know," but Lynn says, "Shit, that girl just *walked* off, I think" (237), leaving everything behind on purpose. The one who is found dead is John, the beloved son of Marty, who has done everything right only to lose the most important thing in his life. Henry, on the other hand, seems to have come through his emotional ordeal at the end of the novel. There is no wife in sight at his house, and he comes to town for the purpose of mailing a stiff, legal-sized envelope, presumably connected with his divorce.

The novel's ending also depends on a Hemingwayesque omission. Mamet has made a good deal of an item that Henry buys at a gun show, a green-and-white patch depicting a fish jumping, which reads "Minnesota Fish and Game—1946." Henry sews it to his hunting jacket with his spare compass beneath it, and when Marty sees him hunting in the woods, he catches "the flash of an embroidered patch high on his jacket" (196). Later, when Henry gets lost in the woods, he cuts off the patch with his knife in order to get at the compass underneath. At the end of the novel, Bill tells Lynn that Marty had given him a patch at his son's funeral, "Fish and *Game* patch [. . .] Minnesota" (236–37), suggesting that it could be a clue to Maris's disappearance. This is the source of Bill's theory that she was killed by an out-of-towner. Does Marty know that this is Henry's patch? Is it possible that Henry has had something to do with Maris's disappearance? Is this a red herring or a clue? Knowing Mamet's penchant for such things (*The Spanish Prisoner, The Cryptogram*), the former seems likely. The patch is a reminder of our inability to solve the deepest riddles of human behavior through such things as clues and reasoning. No one in the village really knew Maris, particularly not Bill, and no one is going to penetrate her mystery by using conventional clues such as this one, which, in pointing toward Henry, so obviously leads in the wrong direction. Everyone in the village is in this sense lost in the woods, just like Henry.

The Old Religion, 1997

Mamet's second novel is a roman à clef based on the trial of Leo Frank for the murder of Mary Phagan. In 1913 Frank was the twenty-nine-year-old supervisor of the National Pencil Factory in Atlanta, a post he had held for almost five years. Although he was born in Texas, he had grown up in Brooklyn and was educated at the Pratt Institute and Cornell University. He had been invited by the owners to come to Atlanta to run the factory. By 1913 he was a well-known businessman in the community and the president of the

Atlanta chapter of B'nai B'rith. Mary Phagan was a thirteen-year-old worker at the factory. On 26 April 1913 she came to the factory to pick up her wages on her way to the Confederate Memorial Day parade. According to Frank, he paid her shortly after noon and never saw her again.

Phagan's body was found at 3:00 A.M. the next day by the night watchman, Newt Lee. Two barely literate notes purporting to be written by Phagan were found near the body. They stated that the murder was done by a "long tall negro black that who is was long sleam negro,"[10] which pointed toward Lee. After questioning various people about the murder, the police arrested Frank and Lee. The day after his arrest, the police dispersed a white mob that threatened to lynch Newt Lee. Jim Conley, a sweeper at the factory and also African American, was arrested after he was found trying to rinse the bloodstains out of a shirt in the factory basement. Only Frank was indicted for the murder. During the trial Conley admitted to writing the notes, but he said that it was Frank who had done the murder and that he had bribed him to write the notes and help him dispose of the body. Frank was convicted of the murder, despite contradictions in Conley's story and the lack of any material evidence against Frank. In the hands of the prosecutor, Hugh Dorsey, the already notorious case became a matter of believing a lurid tale by a humble black man, well-coached in his subservient testimony by the prosecution, or the denial by a Jewish Yankee carpetbagger, against whom the prosecution had paraded witnesses who attested to his unwanted sexual advances to the young women who worked in the factory and suggested that he was a sexual deviant. In their closings Dorsey said that Frank had dishonored the great names in Jewish history through his deviant behavior, and the defense said that Frank was the latest in a long line of Jews who were persecuted for their religious beliefs. The jury convicted Frank. He was sentenced to death, and his lawyers' many appeals were denied.

On 20 June 1915, his last day in office, Georgia governor John Slaton, having spent many hours examining the case, expressed his conviction that Frank was innocent. He was joined in his opinion by the judge who had presided over the case and by Jim Conley's own attorney. Slaton commuted Frank's sentence to life in prison and quickly left the state under police protection. In the middle of the night of 21 June, Frank was transferred from the county prison, which was felt to be vulnerable to a lynch mob, to the Georgia State Penitentiary in Milledgeville, about one hundred miles away. On 18 July, Frank's throat was slashed by another inmate while he was sleeping there, but his life was saved by the efforts of two doctors who also were inmates. A month later, on 16 August, a caravan of cars carrying twenty-five

armed men from Atlanta who called themselves the "Knights of Mary Phagan" surprised the guards at the prison, cut the telephone lines, and kidnaped
Frank, taking him the one hundred miles back to Marietta, Georgia, Mary
Phagan's hometown, fifteen miles from Atlanta, where they lynched him
before a large crowd that had already gathered for the occasion. Frank
asserted his innocence to the end, requesting only that his wedding ring be
returned to his wife. People at the scene began to cut off pieces of his cloth-
ing for souvenirs and to mutilate the body, but they were stopped by a former
judge who was part of the crowd. Although photographs of the scene, one of
which became a souvenir postcard, were readily available, no one was ever
prosecuted for the kidnaping and murder of Leo Frank. The Knights of Mary
Phagan thus became the new invisible order of the Ku Klux Klan, and the
Anti-Defamation League of B'nai B'rith was founded in response to the Leo
Frank case.[11]

The final stroke in this gruesome story came in 1982, when Alonzo Mann,
who had been a thirteen-year-old office boy at the time of the Phagan murder,
unburdened himself of a secret he had kept for sixty-nine years. He had seen
Jim Conley carrying Phagan's body on the first floor of the factory, a fact that
contradicted Conley's testimony and affirmed Frank's. After Mann passed
several lie-detector tests, the story was published by the *Tennessean*. In 1986
the Georgia Board of Pardons and Paroles issued a posthumous pardon to
Leo Frank.

In writing his novel, David Mamet was not so much interested in recount-
ing the events of the case as in exploring the subjective reality of Leo Frank as
he experienced it. He told Charlie Rose that the book was "very, very much
an interior monologue [. . .] It's a fellow who's put in a position where he's
done nothing wrong, and in an attempt to find out, therefore, why he's being
punished, he has to begin examining the nature of the world." Frank is
brought face to face with the essential questions: "What does it mean? What
is justice? What is God? What is reason? What can a good man reasonably
expect? Is he a good man? What is the definition of a good man? And he
has—one of the paths that he takes is to toy with and subsequently embrace
his own invented brand of Judaism."[12] At the same time that the novel represents Frank's subjective experience as he wrestles with these questions, "it's a
book about race hatred," as Mamet has said, and one of the things that Frank
"experiments with in an attempt to explain to himself a world gone mad is
that, perhaps, there is some rectitude in the libels of his accusers," noting that
this is something that many abused people "adopt to deal with intolerable
injustice."[13]

The novel follows the trajectory of Leo's mind as he goes through his trial, imprisonment, and lynching, dealing with the experience first through the evasion of retreating to his memories, and then, as reality becomes too crushing to ignore, moving on to an examination of what is happening to him. The opening chapters of the book contain only brief, occasional hints that Frank is in the midst of his trial. They center on his memories of family life, the life of a family of assimilated Jews in turn-of-the-century Atlanta. The Franks emerge as a close family who are nonobservant religiously but very much rooted in their Jewishness culturally. He thinks of family gatherings at their vacation home on a lake, dominated by the talk of the patriarch, and "the greater benefits of the Leader, in this case, the Father, and the Family Gathering, ruled or commanded or led by a Central Figure."[14] The family discusses the Mortara case, an infamous occurrence in the 1850s, when a boy was taken from his family by the Catholic Church because he had been baptized by a nursemaid and it was not considered fitting for a Christian to be raised by Jews. Morris, the patriarch, tells a joke about anti-Semitism, and there is a discussion of the iconography of a Seder plate. Later, while the family lingers over its Sunday morning breakfast, the neighborhood Christians are returning from church. Frank is "conscious of their position on the back porch, hidden from the road," but he thinks "no, we have the right to be here [. . .] we are not 'screened' from them, for this is where the porch was built; and how could they take umbrage that we've not gone to church. We are not *sequestering* ourselves, for, surely, they can smell our breakfast, and that's the *end* to it" (20).

Frank's habit of mind is reflected in his internal debates about the morality and ethics of the smallest actions, which include wearing a shirt he has promised to give away and buying a watch he does not need, just because it pleases him. He thinks with delight about the annual argument at the Seder table, "for it assured them that they were home. And was that not the point of ritual? [. . .] The point of worth was the liberty to discuss, and, beyond that, below that, the solidarity—the joy of being the same as everyone there, which joy was only underlined by their playing at differences. The argument was their ritual" (44). At the same time, Frank recognizes his "basic, and I could say 'savage,' need to be accepted by the community" (48).

One of the points at which Frank is unable to shut the trial out of his consciousness is when the prosecutor accuses him of Mary Phagan's murder: "She had *rebuffed* you—how many times? And she had learned to *shun* you. And yet you called out, and she turned. And you pushed her down the stairs [. . .] and ravaged her. And beat her. And you took her life.' Frank looked up at the corner of the room" (70). Frank remembers noticing from Mary that day "an odor of uncleanliness" and his thought of "how he'd be hard-pressed to have sex with her, as she smelled unclean. That was the factor, then, perhaps, which buried the memory" (79). Frank felt guilty for having noticed her body, for having thought of it in carnal terms, a feeling that leads him to bury the memory and deny knowing the girl, but also to feel guilt, which is part of what keeps him from asserting his innocence. In the courtroom Frank sits "like an animal" (92). "'If he were innocent, he would rise up and kill the [prosecutor],' one of the reporters thought. 'A man would. *I* would'" (92).

As Frank sits thinking of the ritual torment of the trial, the prosecutor rants against his passivity, his lack of grief and feeling, his lack of humanity. The newspapers had described his feral eyes, his blank look, and his lack of remorse. As the jury embraces "Jim's portrayal of the Happy Slave" (95) in his testimony, it is the Jew who becomes the Other. "Then who was the outsider? The Kike. The 'Nigger to the nth degree'—as the paper had called him—who should have *known* better, having been granted the almost-more-than-provisional status of a White Man" (95). Frank accuses himself of being a fool when he becomes aware that his attorney has no desire to see him acquitted because that decision would subject him to the rage of the city. He just wants to be seen as having put up a valiant effort to show the justice of the system. Frank's low point, however, comes when the description of his genital "deformity"—misinformed reference to circumcision that is made by one of the girls who falsely accuses him of making sexual advances to her—leads to a psychological examination for depravity. The experience has led Frank to a double consciousness, as it is described by W. E. B. Dubois in *The Souls of Black Folk*, his own feeling that his identity has been fatally undermined by his unavoidable sense of the identity imposed on him, the Jewish Other, by the gentile majority—to whom he is monstrous, deformed, animal, furtive, feral.

After recognizing that he has been complicit in allowing himself to be seen as "The Jew," the Other, not only in the trial but in his daily life, Frank goes through a process of trying to discover his true identity. At first he is disappointed in the rabbi who visits him in his cell and helps him with his study of Hebrew and the Torah. He believes that the rabbi, like everyone else, thinks he is guilty and abhors him for making things worse for the Jews. Frank feels an irrational hatred for him. But as the rabbi's visits continue, Frank begins to learn from him, a wisdom imparted through the study of Hebrew words. Finally the rabbi tells him that to be a man "was to behave as a man in that situation where there were neither the trappings nor the rewards of manhood: scorned, reviled, abandoned, humiliated, powerless, terrified, mocked. '*Now* be a man . . .' the Rabbi said" (156). Finding his own personal meaning in

Hebrew words leads to Frank's exploration of Gematria, Hebrew numerology, in order to penetrate to a deeper mystical significance. Frank takes the manufacturer's mark on the bars of his cell, "Ginnett and Hubbard. Penal Engineering. Booth, Ohio," and tries to construct his own cosmology out of the letters. Although recognizing its irrationality, he finds in his occupation a certain sense. "Will I say that these men, Hubbard and Ginnett, were put on the earth to place their names upon that bar to instruct me? No, I will not. Will I say *I* was not put upon the earth to find a meaning in their names? I cannot discount it. For is that not the enterprise in which I find myself? And, if it's ludicrous, how much more so is my incarceration for a crime simple right reason knows me innocent of having done" (168). After this he accepts a certain responsibility for his fate for having unintentionally insulted Jim Conley: "When I saw his eyes, I felt, frankly, I had wronged him. Though *I did not intend to;* and although I regretted it" (183). This is a matter of cause and effect rather than of moral culpability, however, and Frank recognizes this in suggesting that his mistake was not to have fired Conley after this, because one of them had to leave. Instead he kept him on as a result of moral obligation without in the least reducing his enmity.

The futility of calculations such as this is apparent when, after Frank nods to a worker in the prison library, the man comes over and cuts his throat, an expression of calm happiness on his face. Realizing that "all of these people have been told by their God that it is a praiseworthy act to want me dead," Frank "surrendered into madness for a while" (188). Finally he descends to considering the possibility that he is indeed guilty of the murder in order to gain the acceptance of the community: "The one event, if I had misremembered it, could make it right. If I had killed her, if I could avow the fact, then it would all come right. I would be saved" (191). But he wonders, "how could it be that a man would merit his neighbor's love more as a murderer than as a Jew?" (191), and he realizes that if he embraced the Christians, they still would not embrace him.

The book ends with Frank's kidnaping and lynching. Mamet adds the detail that the men castrate him, which is not historically accurate. This departure from the historical record, along with several other changes, underlines Mamet's thematic concerns but also represents Frank as a more conventional victim of anti-Semitism than the historical Leo Frank was. Far from having a passive lawyer who loathed him and did not desire his acquittal, Frank was represented by Luther Rosser, considered "one of the ablest criminal lawyers in the state,"[15] who was joined prior to the trial by the prominent Atlanta attorney Reuben Arnold, who issued a well-publicized statement that he had reviewed all the evidence and had become convinced of Frank's innocence. They aggressively pursued appeals of the verdict all the way to the U.S. Supreme Court. Mamet also presents a negative image of Frank's wife as obese. "It was the grossness of his wife, he knew, which upset them. Her weight" (104), Frank thinks, and "they looked at her as they would at a sow" and at him as "the invert who did what with that gross woman behind him" (105). The historical Lucille Frank was a little overweight, but not remarkably so. She appears calm and fashionably dressed in pictures from the trial, the image of the loyal and supportive wife she apparently was. Mamet also moved the prison stabbing from the dormitory, where Frank was stabbed in his sleep, to the library, where he is stabbed by a fellow inmate with whom he had just attempted to make friendly contact.

The major departure from the historical record, however, is in the character of Leo Frank himself, whom Mamet represents as completely passive, so overcome by his ordeal that he is incapable of engaging in his own defense, or even of responding to questions, as in the incident with the doctor. The historical Leo Frank spoke for more than four hours when called on to do so in the trial, gave an eloquent speech when asked if he had anything to say at his sentencing, and wrote newspaper articles and held press conferences in jail. On 2 March 1914 he told a *New York Times* reporter, "a human life is at stake. That it happens to be mine is incidental. It actually is an incident in my view of the case. The big principles involved are the things that count and not a person's identity. What I say and what I feel are from the viewpoint of a person totally separated from actual connection with the tragedy and its investigation [. . .] I say to every man, woman, and child in Georgia that I am innocent of the charges brought against me. If I had not said it so many times, I would repeat that the hand that wrote the notes was the hand that strangled Mary Phagan."[16] On 27 February, after asking that the Atlanta reporters be assembled in the jail, he told them, "I don't ask for sympathy. I don't need sympathy. What I want is a square deal, and I haven't had it yet [. . .] I have not yet lost faith in human honesty [. . .] and I believe that the people of Georgia will see to it that I am given justice in the end." Speaking of the prosecutor, Hugh Dorsey, he said "It is a terrible thing to suggest that a public official would advance his prestige at the expense of an innocent man's life. And yet— you can see how it is. There is not much glory to be gained by convicting a negro of a sensational crime."[17] The forthright, even aggressive man whom these lines evoke is far from the passive, introverted Leo Frank who appears in *The Old Religion*. The novel's protagonist is Mamet's creation, and he serves Mamet's ends, but he may in the end be a reinscription of the Jew as passive victim. The historical Leo Frank may in the end be a more complex and interesting figure than Mamet's character.

Wilson: A Consideration of the Sources, 2001

If *The Old Religion* is a modernist monologue, *Wilson* is a postmodern pastiche. It consists of a series of fragmentary documents—diary entries, poems and songs, scholarly articles, blurbs from book jackets, government pamphlets, joke books, pages from novels, children's books, advice manuals, and so on—that have been heavily annotated by several generations of scholars, accumulating footnote on footnote. The "real time" of the novel occurs a few centuries in the future. Most of the earth's culture has been lost in the collapse of the Internet in 2021, since books and papers had all been digitized and resided only in cyberspace, and shortly afterward the earth descended into chaos in the "Cola Riots," which were incited by the populace's discovery that Coke and Pepsi were the same thing. Some people have escaped to Mars, and a small collection of fragments from the old culture that were in a capsule have survived and been appropriately placed in a museum, where they are studied endlessly by scholars. Recurring figures in the fragments include the lovers Chet and Donna; Ginger, a sort of hard-boiled young woman who is in a mental hospital, identifies with Woodrow Wilson's wife Edith, and may have killed Chet and Donna; Edith Wilson herself; the Toll Hound, a dog who is said to have danced when he saw the capsule landing, but who may have been imaginary; the Old Wrangler, a character in old Westerns who has been mythicized; Jane of Trent, a writer; Bootsie, who may be a rabbit; and the Bootsie Club, which exists "to impart to its members a feeling of connection to the past, in studying the arcana, in trading artefacts and in the search for relics, its members engaged in . . . benign and fond ancestor worship."[18]

Reviewers of the book generally did not know what to make of it. It was called an "unruly anti-novel [. . .] a futurist-modernist text of sorts," a "futurist, dystopian look at the structure of consciousness [. . .] a decentered narrative organized in fragments with an indeterminate plot written upon by intruding references," and an "imitation of a scholarly work [. . .] closer to the nonsense verse of Edward Lear—if Lear had taken acid and been an avid reader of Penthouse Forum."[19] It was generally agreed, however, that the novel belonged to the genre known as "scholar fiction," following in the wake of Vladimir Nabokov's *Pale Fire* and gesturing back as far as Alexander Pope's *Dunciad.* The spirit of academic parody certainly pervades this book, with its send-up of academic methods, particularly given the academics' needless display of erudition and their smug assumption that what they are doing is worthwhile.

Mamet's parodic efforts range from silly puns to hilarious satire. Factual errors abound, undermining the whole superstructure of commentary by which the scholars live. One pamphlet says "we have been told 'Abraham Lincoln' wrote the Gettysburg Address on the back of an elephant" and is footnoted with "Envelope? Disputed" (143), which leads to a scholarly inquiry as to whether this was the corruption of a text reading the "lack" of an elephant and a discussion of the utility of elephants in the Civil War. Writing of the crash of the Internet and the riots, one scholarly text suggests: "For, dating the birth of Edison in 1941, and the Crash of the Internet in 2021, we have a period of eighty or, in the words of the phone book, 'four score, thank you for calling' years of the reign of that commodity understood as 'information,' we have a scant nineteen years, the 'time of the Troubles,' before the Revelation, and the Riots" (20–21). A good example of the parodies of academic scholarship is an article entitled "Let us Consider the 'Wobbly,'" which is an explication of the "Song of the Wobbly Hung from the Bridge": "Gone off to meet Joe Hill, / Gone off to meet Joe Hill. / Worked my life worried, and I'm worried still. / Gone off to meet Joe Hill" (45). After listing the facts "im- and explicit in the verse itself," such as that the Wobbly has spent his or her life worried and is going to meet Joe Hill, the article goes into a discussion of lynching, and then notes a branch of scholarship that identifies the Wobbly with the Toll Hound: "Was it because the Toll Hound danced? Was the tradition based upon the merest association of 'dance' and gyration ('wobbling')"?

> *Might* the Toll Hound have hung from a bridge?
> *Might* the Toll Hound have been "worried"?
> May we consider dancing *work*?
> Who was Joe Hill? (46)

The argument then goes on to suggest that Joe Hill was a corruption of John Peel, the master of foxhounds in the eighteenth-century ballad "D-ye Ken John Peel with His Coat So Gay." The hound becomes a personification of a hill, and the suggestion is made that musicologists might consider the "*virtual identity* of the song 'John Peel' and the twentieth-century jingle 'Pepsi Cola hits the spot' (1950–1960, and resurfacing, of course, as 'The Song of the Republicans' during the early days of the Riots)" (47).

The book contains pages and pages of such "analysis," but Mamet's satire, as blunt a weapon as it is, has a more specific goal than simply taking potshots at academia. The reader is almost forced by the accumulation of such things into the contemplation of the impossibility of ever understanding the present, let alone reconstructing the past from the random shards and fragments that happen to survive. A fragment called "Lost" reflects several Mametesque ideas about the past. "It has been said that the *past* does not change. What bullshit. How can we say that it does not change, if it is (*as* it is) unknowable?" (128), says the unknown writer. A brief statement sums up the view of historical scholarship that is demonstrated to a fault in the book: "The 'past,' reflection will reveal, is merely *our idea* of what happened. It has no connection whatever to the (should they, in fact, exist) actual events which have (perhaps) transpired. Even were we not manipulated by an outside (human) force, our memory is imperfect, our methods of recording liable to decay, loss and mistranscription (let alone analysis)" (129).

As might be expected in a postmodern novel, *Wilson* has another dimension that is animated by the spirit of play in the puzzles and cryptograms that are dear to Mamet's heart. The text is full of puzzles and codes, from "psycho-numerology" to something called the "Inner Code," originating in a comic-book puzzle for children, which may or may not exist, to the cryptogram that Mrs. Wilson is said to have written in her own urine and thrown out the window, to the acrostics in the poem that both begins and ends the volume. There are references to the various puzzles, particularly the acrostics, which spell out "TOLL HOUN" and "DFSS," and Mrs. Wilson's "DFJJ" throughout the book, with varying attempts to explain them. Toward the end it is suggested by the iconic scholar, Greind, who is referred to elsewhere as a suicide, that his colleague Bennigsen hoped there "would be found that fragment which would make the whole thing whole" and that others have suggested that "Bennigsen was *himself* the 'missing page'; that it was only in his 'self' that the disparate elements were 'made whole'" (313). This brings a note of hope and humanity to a landscape that is otherwise deeply dystopian and characterized by madness, suicide, murder, imprisonment, and death. The reader cannot help but be skeptical of such a reading. If Mamet loves a cryptogram, he loves a con job more, and it is the spirit of the con that looms over this world. Among human beings, the fragment suggests:

> The individual lauded as most prescient is not him of the greatest intelligence, but him with the most power to convince.
> So, it was that combination which led to the species' demise.
> Their intelligence enabled them (potentially) to assess and withstand a threat.
> But the survival of the herd instinct led them to squander any advantage in obedience to (what they each hoped was) the will of the group. (314)

This is familiar ground for Mamet. If academia is one giant con aimed at duping people into believing that scholars have the key to understanding an inexplicable world, whether the past or the present, it is the desire of human beings to be duped that leaves them vulnerable. There is nothing in *Wilson* that suggests the fragments that we know as human culture can be made into something whole or understandable, entertaining as it may be to try.

NOTES

Chapter 1—Understanding David Mamet

1. Stephen Whitty, "Mamet Speaks," (Newark) *Star Ledger*, 29 April 1998, sec. 4: 1.

2. Marilyn Stasio, "Hunting the Buffalo," *Cue*, 19 March–1 April 1977, n.p.

3. Jan Holdenfield, "A Ping-Pong Hustler Writes a Play," *New York Post*, 3 March 1977, Entertainment sec.: 12.

4. David J. Blum, "David Mamet's Wealth of Words," *Wall Street Journal*, 11 June 1982, 25.

5. Jennifer Allen, "David Mamet's Hard Sell," *New York*, 9 April 1984, 40.

6. Whitty, "Mamet Speaks," 1.

7. Andrew Billen, "Man on a Knife Edge," (London) *Evening Standard*, 27 October 1999, 29.

8. Ibid.

9. Simon Houpt, "Hollywood's Con Artist," (Toronto) *Globe and Mail*, 19 December 2000, R1.

10. Marcus Dunk, "America's Hard Man of Letters," *Express*, 26 February 2000, posted 13 April 2000, www.lexisnexis.com.

11. Ira Nadel, *David Mamet: A Life in the Theatre* (New York: Palgrave, Macmillan, 2008), 18.

12. Matthew C. Roudané, "Something Out of Nothing," in Leslie Kane, ed., *David Mamet in Conversation,* 50 (Ann Arbor: University of Michigan Press, 2001).

13. David Mamet, *Glengarry Glen Ross* (New York: Grove, 1984), 96.

14. Blum "David Mamet's Wealth of Words," 25.

15. Bruce Weber, "At 50, a Mellower David Mamet May Be Ready to Tell His Story," *New York Times*, 16 November 1997, AR12.

16. Ibid.

17. Ibid.

18. John Lahr, "Betrayals," *New Yorker* (1 August 1994): 73.

19. David Mamet, *The Wicked Son: Anti-Semitism, Self-Hatred, and the Jews* (New York: Nextbook/Shocken, 2006), xi–xii.

Chapter 2—The Essays

1. David Mamet, *Some Freaks* (New York: Viking, 1989), 86. Subsequent page references appear in the text.

2. David Mamet, *Writing in Restaurants* (New York: Viking-Penguin, 1986), 88–89. Subsequent page references appear in the text.

3. David Mamet, "Deer Hunting," *Make-Believe Town* (Boston: Little, Brown, 1996), 106–7, 108.

4. David Mamet, *Jafsie and John Henry* (New York: Free Press, 1999), 170. Subsequent page references appear in the text.

5. Interestingly Lynn Mamet forgave her stepfather, while David never did. Bernard Kleiman went on to have a long and distinguished legal career representing the United Steelworkers Union as its general counsel. In his 2006 obituary in the Pittsburgh *Post-Gazette*, Lynn is listed among the family members who survived him; David is not.

6. David Mamet, *True and False: Heresy and Common Sense for the Actor* (New York: Vintage, 1997), 3. Subsequent page references appear in the text.

7. David Mamet, *The Wicked Son: Anti-Semitism, Self-Hatred, and the Jews* (New York: Nextbook/Schocken 2006), x. Subsequent page references appear in the text.

8. Jordan Hiller, "The Wicked Son by David Mamet," http://www.bangitout.com, posted 26 January 2007. Accessed 22 December 2010.

9. Lawrence Bush, "The Wicked Witch and the Straw Man," http://Forward.com, posted 22 September 2006. Accessed 22 December 2010.

10. Shaun Smith, "The Only Good Jew is a Very Angry Jew," *Toronto Star*, 1 April 2007, D6.

11. Bush, "The Wicked Witch and the Straw Man."

12. Joe Eskenazi, "'The Wicked Son' by David Mamet," http://www.beyondchron .org, posted 16 November 2006. Accessed 22 December 2010.

13. Ibid.

14. Sanford Pinsker, "David Mamet, Scold," http://www.jbooks.com/nonfiction/index/NF_Pinsker_Mamet.htm. Accessed 22 December 2010.

15. Eskenazi, "'The Wicked Son' by David Mamet."

16. Bush, "The Wicked Witch and the Straw Man."

17. David Mamet, "Why I Am No Longer a Brain-Dead Liberal," *Village Voice*, posted 11 March 2008, www.villagevoice.com. Accessed 22 December 2010.

18. "David Mamet Grows Up," *New Criterion* 26 (April 2008): 3.

19. Dinesh D'Souza, "David Mamet Leaves the Brain Dead Left," http://townhall .com, posted 6 October 2008. Accessed 22 December 2010.

Chapter 3—Men with Men, Women with Women

1. David Radavich, "Man among Men: David Mamet's Social Order," *American Drama* 1, no. 1 (1991): 46–60.

2. Mark Zweigler, "Solace of a Playwright's Ideals," in Leslie Kane, ed., *David Mamet in Conversation*, 17 (Ann Arbor: University of Michigan Press, 2001).

3. Matthew C. Roudané, "Something Out of Nothing," in Leslie Kane, ed., *David Mamet in Conversation*, 50 (Ann Arbor: University of Michigan Press, 2001).

4. The text referred to here and in subsequent page references is that in the volume *The Woods, Lakeboat, Edmond* (New York: Grove, 1987). This version, revised for the Milwaukee Repertory Production directed by John Dillon in 1980, is the text of the first published version. The 1983 Samuel French acting edition incorporates some changes made for later productions, including an additional scene.

5. Sheridan Morley, revision of *Lakeboat, Theatre Record*, 29 (January–11 February 1998): 128.

6. C. W. E. Bigsby, *David Mamet* (London and New York: Methuen, 1985), 26.

7. Ibid., 22–23.

8. Michael Hinden, "'Intimate Voices': *Lakeboat* and Mamet's Quest for Community," in Leslie Kane, ed., *David Mamet: A Casebook,* 33–48 (New York: Garland, 1992).

9. Johan Callens, "The 1970s," in Christopher Bigsby, ed., *The Cambridge Companion to David Mamet,* 42 (Cambridge: Cambridge University Press, 2004).

10. Alain Piette, "The 1980s," in Bigsby, ed., *The Cambridge Companion to David Mamet,* 76.

11. For an extended analysis of the mentor relationship see Pascale Hubert-Leibler, "Dominance and Anguish: The Teacher-Student Relationship in the Plays of David Mamet," in Kane, ed., *David Mamet in Conversation,* 69–85.

12. Quoted in Charlie Rose, "A Great Longing to Belong," transcript of *The Charlie Rose Show.* WNET New York, 11 November 1997, in Kane, ed., *David Mamet in Conversation,* 186.

13. David Mamet, *Sexual Perversity in Chicago and The Duck Variations* (New York: Grove, 1978), 73.

14. David Mamet, *The Cabin: Reminiscence and Diversions* (New York: Turtle Bay, 1992), 96.

15. Ibid., 98.

16. Quoted in Ernest Leogrande, "A Man of Few Words Moves on to Sentences," in Kane, ed., *David Mamet in Conversation,* 28.

17. See Bigsby, *The Cambridge Companion to David Mamet,* 27, and Dennis Carroll, *David Mamet* (London: Macmillan, 1987), 72.

18. David Mamet, *The Disappearance of the Jews, The Old Neighborhood: Three Plays* (New York: Vintage, 1998), 13. Subsequent page references appear in the text.

19. Jeremy McCarter, "A Gay Old Time," *New York Sun,* 22 November 2002, 12.

20. Michael Feingold, "Vagina Dialogues Etc.," *Village Voice,* 27 November–3 December 2002, 66.

21. In 1893 Ednah D. Cheney described a Boston marriage as "the existence of ties between women so intimate and persistent, that they are fully recognised by their friends [. . .] these relations so far as I have known, and I have known many of them, are not usually planned for convenience or economy, but grow out of a constantly increasing attachment, favored by circumstances, which makes such a marriage the best refuge against the solitude of growing age." (Ednah D. Cheney, letter to the editor, *Open Court,* 5 January 1893, 7).

22. David Mamet, *Boston Marriage* (New York: Vintage, 2002), 3. Subsequent page references appear in the text.

23. Charles Isherwood, "Mamet's Distinctive Voice Muffled in Chintz," *Variety,* 2 December 2002, 34.

24. Maurice Charney, "Parody—and Self-Parody in David Mamet," *Connotations* 13, nos. 1–2 (2003–4): 82.

25. Oscar Wilde, *The Importance of Being Earnest,* in *The Complete Works of Oscar Wilde* (Garden City, N.Y. Doubleday, Page, 1923), 21–24. Bunbury is the imaginary invalid friend whom Algernon uses as an excuse to escape his social obligations.

26. David Mamet, *Squirrels* (New York: Samuel French, 1982), 5. Subsequent page references appear in the text.

27. David Mamet, *A Life in the Theatre* (New York: Grove, 1978), 86. Subsequent page references appear in the text.

28. William B. Collins, "Mamet's Tag Line for His Play on Words," (Philadelphia) *Inquirer,* 29 January 1990: D3.

29. David Mamet, *Make-Believe Town: Essays and Remembrances* (Boston: Little, Brown, 1996), 33.

30. David Radavich, "Man among Men: David Mamet's Homosocial Order," *American Drama* 1, no. 1 (1991): 52

31. David Mamet, "A 'Sad Comedy' about Actors." *New York Times,* 16 October 1977, sec. 2: 7.

32. Glenn Loney, "Peter Evans and Ellis Rabb Give Life to the Theater," *After Dark* (February 1978): 78.

Chapter 4—Men and Women

1. David Mamet, *All Men Are Whores,* in *Goldberg Street: Short Plays and Monologues* (New York: Grove, 1985), 199.

2. Quoted in Henry I. Schvey, "Celebrating the Capacity for Self-Knowledge," in Leslie Kane, ed., *David Mamet in Conversation,* 68 (Ann Arbor: University of Michigan Press, 2001).

3. David Mamet, *Sexual Perversity in Chicago and the Duck Variations* (New York: Grove, 1978), 8. Subsequent page references appear in the text.

4. Anne Dean, *David Mamet: Language as Dramatic Action* (Rutherford, N.J.: Fairleigh Dickinson University Press, 1990), 7.

5. Gerald Fraser, "Mamet's Plays Shed Masculinity Myth," *New York Times,* 5 July 1976, 7.

6. Ibid.

7. C. W. E. Bigsby, *Modern American Drama 1945–1990* (Cambridge: Cambridge University Press, 1992), 208.

8. Quoted in Ross Wetzsteon, "David Mamet: Remember That Name," in Kane, ed., *David Mamet in Conversation,* 12.

9. Fraser, "Mamet's Plays Shed Masculinity Myth," 7.

10. Wetzsteon, "David Mamet: Remember That Name," 12.

11. See Douglas Bruster, "David Mamet and Ben Jonson: City Comedy Past and Present," in Bloom, ed., *David Mamet,* 42, and David Skeele, "The Devil and David Mamet: *Sexual Perversity in Chicago* as Homiletic Tragedy" *Modern Drama* 36, no. 4 (1993): 512–18.

12. Skeele, "The Devil and David Mamet," 514–15.

13. Ibid., 517.

14. Bert Cardullo, "Comedy and *Sexual Perversity in Chicago,*" *Notes on Contemporary Literature* 12, no. 1 (1982): 6.

15. Michael Feingold, "Normal Perversions Come to Second City," *Village Voice,* 13 October 1975: 113.

16. Edith Oliver, "David Mamet of Illinois," *New Yorker* 10 Nov. 1975: 136.

17. David Radavich, "Man among Men: David Mamet's Homosocial Order," *American Drama* 1, no. 1 (1991): 47.

18. Fraser, "Mamet's Plays Shed Masculinity Myth," 7.

19. Ibid.

20. Wetzeon, "David Mamet: Remember That Name," 12.

21. Fraser, "Mamet's Plays Shed Masculinity Myth," 7.

22. Dean, *David Mamet,* 18.

23. Schvey, "Celebrating the Capacity for Self-Knowledge," 68.

24. Ibid.

25. David Mamet, *The Woods, Lakeboat, Edmond* (New York: Grove, 1987), 82. Subsequent page references appear in the text.

26. Linda Winer, "Clickety-clack of David Mamet's Typewriter Is Heard through Woods," *Chicago Tribune* 17 Nov. 1977: B6.

27. See C. W. E. Bigsby, *David Mamet* (London and New York: Methuen, 1985), 57–58, and C. W. E. Bigsby, *A Critical Introduction to Twentieth-Century American Drama*, vol. 3, *Beyond Broadway* (Cambridge: Cambridge University Press, 1985), 280.

28. Bigsby, *David Mamet* 58.

Chapter 5—Parents and Children

1. Bruce Weber, "At 50, a Mellower David Mamet May Be Ready to Tell His Story," *New York Times,* 16 November 1997, AR7, 12.

2. Mamet, *Reunion,* in *Reunion, Dark Pony: Two Plays by David Mamet* (New York: Grove Press, 1979), 23. Subsequent page references appear in the text.

3. C. W. E. Bigsby, *Modern American Drama 1945–1990* (Cambridge: Cambridge University Press, 1992), 207.

4. Edward J. Esche, "David Mamet," in Clive Bloom, ed., *American Drama,* 165–77 (New York: St. Martin's, 1995).

5. Michael Hinden, "Intimate Voices: *Lakeboat* and Mamet's Quest for Community," in Leslie Kane, ed., *David Mamet: A Casebook,* 35 (New York: Garland, 1992).

6. Weber, "At 50, a Mellower David Mamet," AR12.

7. Quoted in Jeremy Isaacs, "Face to Face," in Kane, ed., *David Mamet in Conversation,* 215.

8. Leslie Kane, *Weasels and Wisemen: Ethics and Ethnicity in the Work of David Mamet* (New York: St. Martin's Press, 1999), 244–45.

9. David Mamet, *The Old Neighborhood: Three Plays* (New York: Vintage, 1998), 47. Subsequent references appear in the text.

10. Isaacs, "Face to Face," 215.

11. Quoted in John Lahr, "The Art of Theatre XI," in Kane, ed., *David Mamet in Conversation,* 116.

12. Quoted in Melvyn Bragg, "The South Bank Show," in Kane, ed., *David Mamet in Conversation,* 150–51.

13. Lahr, "The Art of Theatre XI," 118.

14. Bragg, "The South Bank Show," 153.

15. David Mamet, *The Cryptogram* (New York: Dramatists Play Service, 1995), 45–46. Subsequent page references appear in the text.

16. John Lahr, "Betrayals," *New Yorker* (1 August 1994): 73.

17. Ibid., 71.

18. In a negative review John Simon referred to the play's form as "dramatic fetishism" (John Simon, "Broadway Goes Off," *New York Magazine* [24 April 1995]: 76). Linda Dorff suggested that "the characters negotiate their relationships to each other through a system of mythical objects that refer to the absent father" (Linda Dorff, "Reinscribing the 'Fairy': The Knife and the Mystification of Male Mythology in *The Cryptogram,*" in Harold Bloom, ed., *David Mamet,* 244 [Philadelphia: Chelsea House, 2004], 244). Gaylord Brewer wrote that "*The Cryptogram* abounds in totems, stage visuals that alternately assist and confound interpretation" (Gaylord Brewer,

"Mamet's Divided Magics: Communion and Duplicity in *The Shawl, The Cryptogram,* and Other Works," *American Drama* 14, no. 2 [2005]: 26).

19. Michael Feingold, "Codehearted," *Village Voice,* 25 April 1995, 97.

20. David Mamet, *The Cabin: Reminiscence and Diversions* (New York: Turtle Bay, 1992), 112. Subsequent page references appear in the text.

21. Lahr, "Betrayals," 73.

22. Feingold, "Codehearted," 97.

23. Jill B. Gidmark, "Violent Silences in Three Works of David Mamet," *Midamerica* 25 (1998): 187.

Chapter 6—Confidence Games

1. See William E. Lenz, *Fast Talk and Flush Times: The Confidence Man as a Literary Convention* (Columbia: University of Missouri Press, 1985); John G. Blair, *The Confidence Man in Modern Fiction: A Rogue's Gallery with Six Portraits* (New York: Barnes & Noble, 1979); Kathleen De Grave, *Swindler, Spy, Rebel: The Confidence Woman in Nineteenth-Century America* (Columbia: University of Missouri Press, 1995); Gary H. Lindberg, *The Confidence Man in American Literature* (New York: Oxford University Press, 1982); Warwick Wadlington, *The Confidence Game in American Literature* (Princeton: Princeton University Press, 1975); Susan Kuhlmann, *Knave, Fool, and Genius: The Confidence Man as He Appears in Nineteenth-Century American Fiction* (Chapel Hill: University of North Carolina Press, 1973).

2. David Mamet, *Writing in Restaurants* (New York: Viking-Penguin, 1986), 90. Subsequent page references appear in the text.

3. Quoted in Matthew C. Roudané, "Something Out of Nothing," in Leslie Kane, ed., *David Mamet in Conversation,* 47 (Ann Arbor: University of Michigan Press, 2001).

4. Blair 12.

5. Mamet, *Writing in Restaurants* 109.

6. Ibid. 109, 108.

7. "Dime Letters Ruled OK," *Rocky Mountain News,* 27 April 1935, 1.

8. David Mamet, *The Water Engine, An American Fable* (New York: Samuel French, 1983), 13. Subsequent page references appear in the text.

9. Roudané, "Something" 46.

10. Quoted in David Savran, "Comics Like Me Always Want to Be Tragedians," in Kane, ed., *David Mamet in Conversation,* 78.

11. Roudané, "Something," 47.

12. Ibid., 46–47.

13. John Lahr, "The Art of Theatre XI," in Kane, ed., *David Mamet in Conversation,* 114.

14. Ibid.

15. Marilyn Stasio, "Hunting the Buffalo," *Cue,* 19 March–1 April 1977, n.p.

16. C. W. E. Bigsby, 1985, *David Mamet* (London and New York: Methuen, 1985), 112.

17. Geoffrey Norman and John Rezek, "Working the Con," in Kane, ed., *David Mamet in Conversation,* 139.

18. Lahr, "The Art of Theatre XI," 112.

19. David Mamet, *Glengarry Glen Ross* (New York: Grove, 1984), 13. Subsequent page references appear in the text.

20. David Worster, "How to Do Things with Salesmen: David Mamet's Speech-Act Play," *Modern Drama* 37 (1994), 386, and Jonathan S. Cullick, "'Always Be Closing': Competition and the Discourse of Closure in David Mamet's *Glengarry Glen Ross*," *Journal of Dramatic Theory and Criticism* 8 (Spring 1994): 24. See also Andrea Greenbaum, "Brass Balls: Masculine Communication and the Discourse of Capitalism," *Journal of Men's Studies* 8 (Fall 1999): 33–43; Anne Dean, *David Mamet: Language as Dramatic Action* (Rutherford, N.J.: Fairleigh Dickinson University Press, 1990); Robert Vorlicky, *Act Like a Man: Challenging Masculinities in American Drama* (Ann Arbor: University of Michigan Press, 1995), 25–56, and Robert Vorlicky, "Men among the Ruins," in Leslie Kane, ed., *David Mamet's* Glengarry Glen Ross: *Text and Performance,* 81–105 (New York: Garland, 1996).

21. Vorlicky, "Men" 83.

22. Jon Tuttle, "'Be What You Are': Identity and Morality in *Edmond* and *Glengarry Glen Ross*," in Kane, *David Mamet's* Glengarry Glen Ross, 164.

23. Dean, *David Mamet,* 209.

24. Roudané, "Something," 48.

25. Quoted in Henry I. Schvey, "Celebrating the Capacity for Self-Knowledge," in Kane, ed., *David Mamet in Conversation,* 64.

26. Schvey, "Celebrating the Capacity for Self-Knowledge," 65.

27. Roudané, "Something," 47.

28. Ibid.

29. Ibid.

30. Greenbaum, "Brass Balls," 40.

31. Samuel G. Freedman, "Theater Returns to Lincoln Center," *New York Times,* 21 December 1985, 15.

32. David Mamet, *The Shawl* (New York: Samuel French, 1985), 20. Subsequent page references appear in the text.

33. Tish Dace, "Hauntings," New York *Native,* 27 Jan.–2 Feb. 1986: 41.

34. Schvey, "Celebrating the Capacity for Self-Knowledge," 66.

35. Ibid.

36. Ibid., 67.

37. David Mamet, *Speed-the-Plow* (New York: Grove, 1988), 23.

38. Philip Kolin, "Performing Scripts in David Mamet's *Speed-the-Plow*," *Notes on Contemporary Literature* 28, no. 5 (1998): 5.

39. Mel Gussow, "Mamet's Hollywood is a School for Scoundrels," *New York Times* 15 May 1988: sec. 2, p. 5.

40. Christopher Bigsby suggests that "the fun is to watch three confidence tricksters each determined to trick each other" (C. W. E. Bigsby, *Modern American Drama 1945–1990,* [Cambridge: Cambridge University Press, 1992] 228). Jeanne-Andrée Nelson, on the other hand, insists on the authenticity of Karen's conversion by the novel (Jeanne-Andrée Nelson, "*Speed-the-Plow* or Seed the Plot: Mamet and the Female Reader," *Essays in Theatre/Etudes Theatrales,* 10 [November 1991]: 77). Tony Stafford suggests that, "whether the 'radiation book' is a fraud or whether it is a meaningful work, one cannot and does not need to know" (Tony Stafford, "*Speed-the-Plow* and *Speed the Plough*: The Work of the Earth," *Modern Drama,* 36 [1993]: 45). Stafford believes that the important thing about Karen's admission is that "it jolts Gould out of his idealism and back to the reality of where it is he works" (45).

41. Jack Kroll, "The Terrors of Tinseltown," *Newsweek* 16 May 1988, 82.

Chapter 7—Degeneration and Descent

1. Quoted in Henry I. Schvey, "Celebrating the Capacity for Self-Knowledge," in Kane, ed., *David Mamet in Conversation*, 65 (Ann Arbor: University of Michigan Press, 2001).

2. David Mamet, *American Buffalo* (New York: Grove, 1977), 31. Subsequent page references appear in the text.

3. Quoted in Matthew C. Roudané, "Something Out of Nothing," in Leslie Kane, ed., *David Mamet in Conversation*, 49 (Ann Arbor: University of Michigan Press, 2001).

4. Henry Hewes, David Mamet, John Simon, and Joe Beruh, "Buffalo on Broadway," in Kane, ed., *David Mamet in Conversation*, 25.

5. Roudané, "Something Out of Nothing," 48.

6. Quoted in Terry Gross, "Someone Named Jack," in Kane, ed., *David Mamet in Conversation*, 161.

7. Schvey 67.

8. Ibid.

9. Ibid.

10. David Mamet, *Oleanna* (New York: Vintage, 1993), epigraph. Subsequent page references appear in the text. Pete Seeger published an English version of this Norwegian folk song in 1955. It was popularized in a version by the Kingston Trio in 1959.

11. Lenke Némath, "Miscommunication and Its Implication in David Mamet's *Oleanna*," *B.A.S. British and American Studies* 2 (1997): 174–75.

12. David Mamet, *Writing in Restaurants* (New York: Viking-Penguin, 1986), 44.

13. An earlier version of the script ended with John's reading a public apology for his behavior. Although he reluctantly allowed Harold Pinter to stage the ending this way in the London production, Mamet strongly preferred the later ending, which he used in both his production and his film of *Oleanna*.

14. Quoted in Charlie Rose, "A Great Longing to Belong," in Kane, ed., *David Mamet in Conversation*, 164.

15. A videotape of the 1993 production of *Oleanna* directed by Mamet is available at the New York Public Library for the Performing Arts.

16. Thomas Goggans, "Laying Blame: Gender and Subtext in David Mamet's *Oleanna*," *Modern Drama* 40 (Winter 1997): 436.

17. David Mamet, *Bambi vs. Godzilla: On the Nature, Purpose, and Practice of the Movie Business* (New York: Pantheon, 2007), 19. Subsequent page references appear in the text.

18. Robert Jean Campbell, M. D., *Psychiatric Dictionary*, 6th ed. (New York: Oxford University Press, 1989), 587.

19. Quoted in John Lahr, "The Art of Theatre XI," in Kane, ed., *David Mamet in Conversation*, 119 (Ann Arbor: University of Michigan Press, 2001).

20. Toby Silverman Zinman, "So Dis Is Hollywood: Mamet in Hell," in *Hollywood on Stage: Playwrights Evaluate the Culture Industry*, ed. Kimball King (New York: Garland, 1997), 101–2.

21. David Mamet, *Bobby Gould in Hell*, in *Oh, Hell!: Two One-Act Plays* (New York: Samuel French, 1991), 9. Subsequent page references appear in the text.

22. Georg Kaiser, *From Morn to Midnight* (New York: Brentano's, 1922)150.

23. Quoted in Mimi Leahey, "David Mamet: The American Dream Gone Bad," *Other Stages*, 4 November 1982: 3.

24. Ibid.

25. Don Shewey, "David Mamet Puts a Dark New Urban Drama on Stage," *New York Times* 24 October 1982: 69.

26. David Mamet, *Edmond*, in *The Woods, Lakeboat, Edmond* (New York: Grove, 1987), 227. Subsequent page references appear in the text.

27. C. W. E. Bigsby, *Modern American Drama 1945–1990* (Cambridge: Cambridge University Press, 1992), 226.

28. Dennis Carroll, *David Mamet* (London: Macmillan, 1987), 103.

29. Richard Brucher, "Prophecy and Parody in *Edmond*," *David Mamet,* ed. Harold Bloom (Philadelphia: Chelsea House, 2004), 230.

30. Shewey, "David Mamet Puts a Dark New Urban Drama on Stage," 69.

31. Bigsby, *Modern American Drama 1945–1990,* 226.

32. Edward Lundin, "Mamet and Mystery," *Publications of the Mississippi Philological Association* (1988): 111.

33. Carroll, *David Mamet* 97.

34. Shewey "David Mamet Puts a Dark New Urban Drama on Stage," 67.

35. Ibid.

Chapter 8—The Novels

1. Melvyn Bragg, "The South Bank Show," in Leslie Kane, ed., *David Mamet in Conversation,* 153 (Ann Arbor: University of Michigan Press, 2001).

2. Ibid., 153, 155.

3. Christopher Bigsby, "David Mamet's Fiction," in Christopher Bigsby, ed., *The Cambridge Companion to David Mamet,* 196 (Cambridge: Cambridge University Press, 2004).

4. Ernest Hemingway, *A Moveable Feast* (New York: Scribner's, 1964), 75.

5. John Lahr, "The Art of Theatre XI," in Kane, ed., *David Mamet in Conversation,* 111.

6. Geoffrey Norman and John Rezek, "Working the Con," in Kane, ed., *David Mamet in Conversation,* 129.

7. David Mamet, *The Village* (Boston: Little, Brown 1994), 6. Subsequent page references appear in the text.

8. Mamet makes it clear that he understands what it is like to sit motionless for hours in a deer stand in "Deer Hunting," in his *Make-Believe Town,* 98–100 (Boston: Little, Brown, 1996).

9. Mamet describes an almost identical experience that happened to him in *South of the Northeast Kingdom* (Washington, D.C.: National Geographic, 2002), 84–85.

10. "Split Court Denies New Trial to Frank," *New York Times* 18 February 1914, 3.

11. Charles Pou's chronology of the Leo Frank case on the University of Georgia Libraries website about the state is one of the most complete and straightforward accounts of the events (http://georgiainfo.galileo.usg.edu/leofrank.htm). Accessed 22 December 2010.

12. Charlie Rose, "A Great Longing to Belong," in Kane, ed., *David Mamet in Conversation,* 184–85.

13. Barbara Shulgasser, "Mountebanks and Misfits," in Kane, ed., *David Mamet in Conversation,* 198.

14. David Mamet, *The Old Religion* (New York: Free Press, 1997), 18. Subsequent page references appear in the text.

15. "Troops Called Out in Phagan Murder," *Daily Telegraph* [Macon, Ga.], 2 May 1913, 9.

16. "Burns Takes A Hand in Frank's Behalf," *New York Times*, 3 March 1914, 1.

17. "'I Don't Need Sympathy, but a Square Deal,' Says Leo Frank in Death Cell," *Ledger-Enquirer* [Columbus, Ga.], 27 February 1914, 11.

18. David Mamet, *Wilson: A Consideration of the Sources* (London: Faber, 2000), 155. Subsequent page references appear in the text.

19. "Wilson: A Consideration of the Sources," *Kirkus Reviews*, 15 September 2001, 1323; Ira Nadel, "Review of Mamet's Wilson," http://mamet.eserver.org/review/2000/wilson.html; accessed 22 December 2010. Jeff Zaleski, "Wilson," *Publishers Weekly*, 24 September 2001, 67.

BIBLIOGRAPHY

Works by David Mamet

PLAYS

American Buffalo. New York: Grove, 1977.

Bobby Gould in Hell in *Oh, Hell!: Two One-Act Plays.* New York: Samuel French, 1991.

Boston Marriage. New York: Vintage, 2002.

The Cryptogram. New York: Dramatists Play Service, 1995.

Edmond. New York: Grove, 1983.

Faustus. New York: Vintage, 2004.

Glengarry Glen Ross. New York: Grove, 1984.

Goldberg Street: Short Plays and Monologues. New York: Grove, 1985. Comprises *Goldberg Street; Cross Patch; The Spanish Prisoner; Two Conversations; Two Scenes; Vermont Sketches; The Dog; Film Crew; Four* A.M.*; The Power Outage; Food; Columbus Avenue; Steve McQueen; Yes; The Blue Hour: City Sketches; A Sermon; Shoeshine; Litko: A Dramatic Monologue; In Old Vermont; All Men Are Whores: An Inquiry*

An Interview. In *Death Defying Acts.* New York: Samuel French, 1996.

Lakeboat. New York: Grove, 1981.

A Life in the Theatre. New York: Grove, 1978.

No One Will Be Immune and Other Plays and Pieces. New York: Dramatists Play Service, 1994. Comprises *Almost Done; Monologue; Two Enthusiasts; Sunday Afternoon; The Joke Code; A Scene—Australia; Fish; A Perfect Mermaid; Dodge; L.A. Sketches; A Life with No Joy in It; Joseph Dintenfass; No One Will Be Immune*

The Old Neighborhood: Three Plays. New York: Vintage, 1998.

Oleanna. New York: Vintage, 1993.

Reunion and Dark Pony: Two Plays by David Mamet. New York: Grove, 1979.

Reunion: Three Plays. New York: Samuel French, 1982.

Revenge of the Space Pandas, or Binky Rudich and the Two-Speed Clock. Woodstock, Ill.: Dramatic Publishing, 1978.

Romance. New York: Vintage, 2005.

Sexual Perversity in Chicago and The Duck Variations. New York: Grove, 1978.

The Shawl. New York: Samuel French, 1985.

Short Plays and Monologues. New York: Dramatists Play Service, 1981. Comprises *The Blue Hour: City Sketches; Prairie du Chien; A Sermon; Shoeshine; Litko: A Dramatic Monologue; In Old Vermont; All Men Are Whores: An Inquiry.*

Speed-the-Plow. New York: Grove, 1988.

Squirrels. New York: Samuel French, 1982.
Three Children's Plays. New York: Grove, 1986.
Three Jewish Plays. New York: Samuel French, 1987. Comprises *The Disappearance of the Jews; Goldberg Street; Luftmensch.*
The Water Engine: An American Fable. New York: Samuel French, 1983.
The Woods. New York: Grove, 1979.
The Woods, Lakeboat, Edmond. New York: Grove, 1987.

ADAPTATIONS

Chekhov, Anton. *The Cherry Orchard.* Adapted from a literal translation by Peter Nelles. New York: Grove, 1986.
———. *The Three Sisters: A Play.* Adapted from a literal translation by Vlada Chernomordik. New York: Grove, 1991.
———. *Uncle Vanya.* Adapted from a literal translation by Vlada Chernomordik. New York: Grove, 1989.
———. "Vint." In *Orchards: Seven Stories by Anton Chekhov and Seven Plays They Have Inspired.* New York: Knopf, 1986. 39–48.
Granville-Barker, Harley. *The Voysey Inheritance.* New York: Vintage, 2005.

POETRY

The Chinaman. New York: Overlook, 1999.
The Hero Pony. New York: Grove Weidenfeld, 1990.
Warm and Cold. Illus. Donald Sultan. New York: Grove, 1988.

CHILDREN'S BOOKS

Bar Mitzvah. Illus. Donald Sultan. New York: Little, Brown, 1999.
The Duck and the Goat. Illus. Maya Kennedy. New York: St. Martin's, 1996.
Henrietta. Illus. Elizabeth Dahlie. Boston: Houghton Mifflin, 1999.
The Owl, with Lindsay Crouse. Illus. Stephen Alcom. New York: Kipling, 1987.
Passover. Illus. Michael McCurdy. New York: St. Martin's, 1995.

NONFICTION PROSE

The Audition Monologue: A Practical Guide for Actors. With Karen Kohlhaas. New York: Atlantic Theatre Company, 2000.
Bambi vs. Godzilla: On the Nature, Purpose, and Practice of the Movie Business. New York: Pantheon, 2007.
The Cabin: Reminiscence and Diversions. New York: Turtle Bay, 1992.
Five Cities of Refuge: Weekly Reflections on Genesis, Exodus, Leviticus, Numbers, and Deuteronomy. With Lawrence Kushner. New York: Schocken, 2003.
Jafsie and John Henry. New York: Free Press, 1999.
Make-Believe Town: Essays and Remembrances. Boston: Little, Brown, 1996.
Notes for a Catalogue for Raymond Saunders. With Raymond Saunders. San Francisco: Stephen Wirtz Gallery, 1985.
On Directing Film. New York: Viking-Penguin, 1991.
Some Freaks. New York: Viking, 1989.
South of the Northeast Kingdom. Washington, D.C.: National Geographic Society, 2002.
Theatre. New York: Faber and Faber, 2010.

True and False: Heresy and Common Sense for the Actor. New York: Pantheon, 1997.
Three Uses of the Knife: On the Nature and Purpose of Drama. New York: Columbia University Press, 1998. Reprint, New York: Vintage, 2000.
A Whore's Profession: Notes and Essays. London: Faber, 1994. Comprises *The Cabin; Writing in Restaurants; Some Freaks; On Directing Film.*
The Wicked Son: Anti-Semitism, Self-Hatred, and the Jews. New York: Nextbook/Schocken, 2006.
Writing in Restaurants. New York: Viking-Penguin, 1986.

FICTION

The Old Religion. New York: Free Press, 1997.
The Village. Boston: Little, Brown 1994.
Wilson: A Consideration of the Sources. London: Faber, 2000.

FILM AND TELEVISION

5 Televison Plays. New York: Grove, Weidenfeld, 1990.
Homicide. New York: Grove, Weidenfeld, 1992.
House of Games. New York: Grove, 1985.
The Spanish Prisoner and The Winslow Boy: Two Screenplays. New York: Vintage, 1999.
Things Change. With Shel Silverstein. New York: Grove, 1988.
We're No Angels. New York: Grove, Weidenfeld, 1990.

Secondary Sources

BIBLIOGRAPHIES AND CHECKLISTS

Jones, Nesta and Steven Dykes. *File on Mamet.* London: Methuen, 1991.
Price, Steven. *The Plays, Screenplays and Films of David Mamet: A Reader's Guide to Essential Criticism.* Houndmills, U.K.: Palgrave, 2008.
Sauer, David K. and Janice A. Sauer. *David Mamet: A Research and Production Sourcebook.* Westport, Conn.: Praeger, 2003.

BIOGRAPHIES AND CRITICAL STUDIES

Barton, Bruce. *Imagination in Transition: Mamet's Move to Film.* Bruxelles: P.I.E.-Peter Lang, 2005.
Bigsby, C. W. E.. *David Mamet.* London: Methuen, 1985.
Brewer, Gay. *David Mamet and Film: Illusion/Disillusion in a Wounded Land.* Jefferson, N.C.: McFarland, 1993.
Carroll, Dennis. *David Mamet.* New York: St. Martin's, 1987.
Dean, Anne. *David Mamet: Language as Dramatic Action.* Rutherford, N.J.: Fairleigh Dickinson University Press, 1990.
Geis, Deborah R. *Postmodern Theatric[k]s: Monologue in Contemporary Drama.* Ann Arbor: University of Michigan Press, 1993.
Kane, Leslie. *Weasels and Wisemen: Ethics, and Ethnicity in the Work of David Mamet.* New York: St. Martin's Press, 1999.
McDonough, Carla J. *Staging Masculinity: Male Identity in Contemporary American Drama.* Jefferson, N.C.: McFarland, 1997.
Nadel, Ira. *David Mamet: A Life in the Theatre.* New York: Palgrave Macmillan, 2008.

Sauer, David K. *David Mamet's* Oleanna. New York: Continuum, 2008.

Vorlicky, Robert. *Act Like a Man: Challenging Masculinities in American Drama*. Ann Arbor: University of Michigan, 1995.

COLLECTIONS OF ESSAYS AND INTERVIEWS

Bigsby, Christopher, ed. *The Cambridge Companion to David Mamet*. Cambridge: Cambridge University Press, 2004.

Bloom, Harold, ed. *David Mamet*. Philadelphia: Chelsea House, 2004.

Callens, Johan, ed. *Crossings: David Mamet's Work in Different Genres and Media*. Newcastle upon Tyne: Cambridge Scholars Publishing, 2009.

Hudgins, Christopher C. and Leslie Kane, eds. *Gender and Genre: Essays on Mamet*. New York: Palgrave, 2001.

Kane, Leslie, ed. *The Art of Crime: The Plays and Films of Harold Pinter and David Mamet*. New York: Routledge, 2004.

———. *David Mamet: A Casebook*. New York: Garland, 1992.

———. *David Mamet in Conversation*. Ann Arbor: University of Michigan Press, 2001.

———. *David Mamet's Glengarry Glen Ross: Text and Performance*. New York: Garland, 1996.

SECTIONS OF BOOKS, MAJOR CRITICAL ARTICLES, INTERVIEWS, AND VIDEOS

Individual articles in the collections of essays listed above are not listed here.

Barbera, Jack V. "Ethical Perversity in America: Some Observations on David Mamet's *American Buffalo*." *Modern Drama* 24, no. 3 (1981): 270–75.

Bechtel, Roger. "Acting and the Righteous Man: David Mamet, Bobby Gould, and True and False." *New England Theatre Journal* 17 (2006): 99–119.

———. "P. C. Power Play: Language and Representation in David Mamet's *Oleanna*." *Theatre Studies* 41 (1996): 29–48.

Bigsby, C. W. E. *A Critical Introduction to Twentieth-Century American Drama*. Vol. 3: *Beyond Broadway*. Cambridge: Cambridge University Press, 1985. 251–90.

———. *Modern American Drama: 1945–1990*. Cambridge: Cambridge University Press, 1992. 195–229.

Callens, Johan. "Remediation in David Mamet's *The Water Engine*." *American Drama* 14, no. 2 (2005): 39–55.

Christiansen, Richard. "The Young Lion of Chicago Theater." *Chicago Tribune Magazine* (11 July 1982): sec. 9: 9, 11–14, 18.

Cullick, Jonathan S., "'Always Be Closing': Competition and the Discourse of Closure in David Mamet's *Glengarry Glen Ross*" *Journal of Dramatic Theory and Criticism* 8, no. 2 (1994): 23–36.

Dietrick, Jon. "'Real Classical Money': Naturalism and Mamet's *American Buffalo*." *Twentieth Century Literature* 52, no. 3 (2006): 330–46.

Foster, Verna. "Sex, Power, and Pedagogy in Mamet's *Oleanna* and Ionesco's *The Lesson*." *American Drama* 5, no. 1 (1995): 36–50.

Garner, Stanton B., Jr. "Framing the Classroom: Pedagogy, Power, *Oleanna*." *Theatre Topics* 10, no. 1 (2000): 39–59.

Gidmark, Jill B. "Violent Silences in Three Works of David Mamet." *Midamerica* 25 (1998): 184–92.

Goldensohn, Barry. "David Mamet and Poetic Language in Drama." *Agni* 49 (1999): 139–49.

Goggans, Thomas. "Laying Blame: Gender and Subtext in David Mamet's *Oleanna*." *Modern Drama* 40 (1997), 433–41.

Haedicke, Janet V. "David Mamet: An American on the American Stage." In David Krasner, ed., *A Companion to Twentieth-Century American Drama*, 406–22. Oxford: Blackwell, 2005.

———. "Decoding Cipher Space: David Mamet's *The Cryptogram* and America's Dramatic Legacy." *American Drama* 9.1 (1999): 1–20.

Herman, William. "Theatrical Diversity from Chicago: David Mamet." In Herman's *Understanding Contemporary American Drama*, 125–60. Columbia: University of South Carolina Press, 1987.

Hubert-Leibler, Pascale. "Dominance and Anguish: The Teacher-Student Relationship in the Plays of David Mamet." *Modern Drama* 31, no. 4 (1988): 557–70.

King, Thomas L. "Talk and Dramatic Action in *American Buffalo*." *Modern Drama* 34, no. 4 (1991): 538–48.

Lahr, John. "Betrayals." *New Yorker* 70 (1 August 1994): 70–73.

Little, William. "Taking It Back: Crises of Currency in David Mamet's *American Buffalo*." *Mosaic* 37, no. 3 (2004): 139–55.

MacLeod, Christine. "The Politics of Gender, Language, and Hierarchy in Mamet's *Oleanna*." *Journal of American Studies* 29.2 (1995): 199–213.

Malkin, Jeannette R. *Verbal Violence in Contemporary Drama*. Cambridge: Cambridge University Press, 1992. 145–62.

McDonough, Carla J. "Every Fear Hides a Wish: Unstable Masculinity in Mamet's Drama." *Theatre Journal* 44.2 (1992): 195–205.

Murphy, Brenda. "Williams, Mamet, and the Artist *In Extremis*," In Philip C. Kolin, ed., *The Influence of Tennessee Williams: Essays on Fifteen American Playwrights*, 136–47. Jefferson, N.C.: McFarland, 2008.

Nelson, Jeanne-Andrée. "Speed-the-Plow" or Seed the Plot: Mamet and the Female Reader." *Essays in Theatre / Études théâtrales* 10 (November 1991): 71–82.

Piette, Alain. "The Devil's Advocate: David Mamet's *Oleanna* and Political Correctness." In Marc Maufort, ed., *Staging Difference: Cultural Pluralism in American Theatre and Drama*, 173–87. New York: Peter Lang, 1995.

Porter, Thomas E. "Postmodernism and Violence in Mamet's *Oleanna*." *Modern Drama* 43 (2000): 13–31.

Quinn, Michael L. "Anti-Theatricality and American Ideology: Mamet's Performative Realism." In W. W. Demastes, ed., *Realism and the American Dramatic Tradition*, 235–54. Tuscaloosa: University of Alabama Press 1996.

Radavich, David. "Man among Men: David Mamet's Social Order." *American Drama* 1, no. 1 (1991): 46–60.

Roudané, Matthew C. "Public Issues, Private Tensions: David Mamet's *Glengarry Glen Ross*," *South Carolina Review* 19, no. 1 (1986): 35–47.

Sauer, David Kennedy. "*Oleanna* and *The Children's Hour*: Misreading Sexuality on the Post/Modern Realistic Stage." *Modern Drama* 43.3 (2000): 421–41.

Skeele, David. "The Devil and David Mamet: *Sexual Perversity in Chicago* as Homiletic Tragedy." *Modern Drama* 36, no. 4 (1993): 512–18.

Stafford, Tony J. "*Speed-the-Plow* and *Speed the Plough*: The Work of the Earth." *Modern Drama* 36, no. 1 (1993): 38–47.

Weber, Bruce. "At 50, a Mellower David Mamet May Be Ready to Tell His Story." *New York Times*, 16 November 1997, AR7.

Worster, David. "How to Do Things with Salesmen: David Mamet's Speech-Act Play."
    Modern Drama 37, no. 3 (1994): 375–90.
Zinman, Toby Silverman. "Jewish Aporia: The Rhythm of Talking in Mamet." *The-
    atre Journal* 44, no. 2 (1992): 207–15.
———. "So Dis Is Hollywood: Mamet in Hell," In Kimball King, ed., *Hollywood on
    Stage: Playwrights Evaluate the Culture Industry,* 101–12.
The Playwright Directs. With David Mamet. Videorecording. Written by Stephan
    Chodorov. Directed by John Musili. Kent, Conn.. Creative Arts Television, 1997.

INDEX

Albee, Edward, 27
All about Eve (film), 84
All Men Are Whores, 5, 44, 45
American Buffalo, 1, 10, 22, 26, 64, 79, 81, 89–93; Broadway production of, 5; Mamet on meaning of, 91, 93; as tragedy, 89, 93; Veblenian view of capitalism in, 90
American Tragedy, An (Dreiser), 102
Aristotle, 1, 17, 34, 82
Arnold, Reuben, 118
Asperger's disorder, 97–99

Bambi vs. Godzilla: On the Nature, Purpose, and Practice of the Movie Business, 11, 98
Beckett, Samuel, 27
Bentley, Eric, 46
Bigsby, Christopher (C. W. E.), 23, 25, 46, 58, 60, 105, 106, 109, 129 n. 40
Billen, Andrew, 2
Blair, John, 70
Bobby Gould in Hell, 9, 100
Boston Marriage, 9, 31–37, 44, 52; charges of misogyny in, 31; class in, 36 dialogue in, 32; lesbian subculture in, 34; Oscar Wilde's influence on, 32, 35; parodic elements of, 33–35
Brando, Marlon, 109, 110
Brecht, Bertholt, 1
Brucher, Richard, 105
Büchner, Georg, 101
Butler, Samuel, 94

Cabin, The, 9, 11, 14
Cabot, Vermont, 3, 5, 8, 9, 18, 108, 109

Callens, Johan, 25
CAMEL/A Review, 4, 22
Cardullo, Bert, 47
Carroll, Dennis, 105, 106
Charney, Maurice, 33
Chaucer, Geoffrey, 69
Chekhov, Anton, 6, 7, 16
Cheney, Ednah D., 125 n. 21
Cherry Orchard, The (Chekhov), 7
Compton-Burnett, Ivy, 33
confidence games, 69–70, 87–88
Confidence Man: His Masquerade, The, 69
Conley, Jim, 114, 115
Cox, Patricia, 4
Crouse, Lindsay (former wife), 5, 14, 61, 81
Crouse, Russell, 5
Cryptogram, The, 9, 44, 52, 59, 61, 63–68, 113; Mamet on, 63–64; puzzles in, 64, 65; staircase in, 65–66; symbolism in, 66–68; tragedy in, 64;
Curtiz, Michael, 7

Dark at the Top of the Stairs, The, 65, 66
Dark Pony, 5, 59, 61
de Niro, Robert, 8
Dean, Anne, 45, 51, 77
Death of a Salesman (Miller), 74, 91
Deeny, 8
Diagnostic and Statistical Manual of Mental Disorders, 98
Disappearance of the Jews, The, 8, 22, 30; Jewish identity in, 30
Dorsey, Hugh, 114, 119
Dreiser, Theodore, 102

D'Souza, Dinesh, 20
Dubois, W. E. B., 117
Duck Variations, The, 4, 5, 22, 26–30;
  dialogue in, 27, 28; life cycle in, 29,
  30; writing of, 26, 27
Dunciad, The (Pope), 120

Earplay, 70
Edmond, 6, 8, 70, 90, 101–7; confi-
  dence games in, 103; dialogue in, 105;
  film of, 106; influences on, 101–2;
  Mamet on meaning of, 102, 107;
  monetary exchange in, 102; produc-
  tion of, 106
Eisenstadt, Debra, 99
Emerson, Ralph Waldo, 77
Epictetus, 1
Esche, Edward J., 60
Evans, Peter, 42

Fantasticks, The (Schmidt and Jones), 4,
  41
Faustus, 100–101
Feingold, Michael, 31, 47, 65, 68
Firbank, Ronald, 33
Fox, William, 98
Francis Parker School, 4, 26
Frank, Anne, 10, 18
Frank, Leo Max, 8, 108, 113–16, 118,
  119
Frank, Lucille, 119
Friedman, Milton, 10
From Morn to Midnight (Kaiser), 101
Front Page, The (film), 79

Glass Menagerie, The (Williams), 62
Glengarry Glen Ross, 2, 4, 6, 7, 22, 26,
  70, 72–80, 81, 84, 90, 101; ending of,
  79, 80
genre of, 79; Mamet on the American
  Dream in, 73; Mamet's work back-
  ground for, 73
Goddard College, 4, 6, 22, 26
Goggans, Thomas, 97
Goldwyn, Samuel, 98
Goodman Theatre, 4, 6, 80
Greenbaum, Andrea, 80
Gussow, Mel, 84

Heist, 8, 69
Hemingway, Ernest, 6, 12, 109, 110
Higgins, Michael, 61
Hinden, Michael, 24, 25, 61
Homicide, 8
Hooper, James Jones, 69
House of Games, 5, 7, 69, 70, 82, 83
Huffman, Felicity, 8–10
Importance of Being Earnest, The
  (Wilde), 33, 34
Inge, William, 65, 66, 68
Isherwood, Charles, 33

Jafsie and John Henry, 11, 13, 67
James, Henry, 33
Jay, Ricky, 8, 69
"Jews in Show Business," 98
Johnson, Paul, 20
Johnston, J. J., 8
Jolly, 3, 8, 9, 59, 61–63; as memory
  play, 62–63

Kaiser, Georg, 101
Kane, Leslie, 61
Kimbrough, Linda, 8
Kleiman, Bernard (stepfather), 3, 14,
  15, 124 n. 5
Kleiman, David (stepbrother), 3
Kleiman, Lenore Silver (Mamet;
  mother), 3, 14, 15
Kleiman, Leslie (stepsister), 3
"Knives," 67
Kroll, Jack, 84
Ku Klux Klan, 115
Kuhlmann, Susan, 69

Laemmle, Carl, 98
Lahr, John, 9, 64, 65, 68, 73
Lakeboat, 6, 22–26; dialogue in, 26;
  misogyny in, 25; narrative in, 23–25
"Law of Life, The," 28, 29
Lee, Newt, 114
Life in the Theater, A, 10, 22, 26,
  38–39, 41–43; gay subtext of, 42;
  mentorship in, 41–42
Life with Father (Lindsay and Crouse),
  5
Lindsay, Howard, 5

London, Jack, 6, 28, 29, 111
Lone Canoe, The, 6
Ludlam, Charles, 33

Macy, William H., 1, 4, 8, 16; in
  Oleanna, 97
Madonna, 84
Make-Believe Town, 11
Mamet, Bernard (father), 3, 59
Mamet, Bobby (stepbrother), 3
Mamet, Clara (daughter), 8
Mamet, David Alan: birth of, 3; on capitalism, 90, 101; charges of misogyny
  against, 25, 31, 51; on confidence
  games, 69; Chicago writing of, 4;
  childhood, 3, 9, 14, 15; dialogue of,
  5–7, 26, 89, 90; education of, 4;
  humor of, 26; on hunting, 13; on
  Jewish identity, 17, 18, 20; and
  Judaism, 3, 8, 17; literary influences
  on, 27; on masculine activities, 11,
  12; on the Method, 16; New York
  experience of, 5; parents' divorce, 3;
  sales jobs of, 73; tragedies of, 64
Mamet, Lynn (sister), 3, 9, 14, 15, 59,
  61, 62, 124 n. 5; abusive childhood
  of, 62
Mamet, Noah (son), 8
Mamet, Tony (stepbrother), 3, 8
Mamet, Willa (daughter), 5
Mamet, Zosia (daughter), 5
Mametspeak, 6, 7, 89
Mann, Alonzo, 115
Mantegna, Joe, 8
Marlboro College, 4, 22
Mayer, Louis B., 98
McCarter, Jeremy, 31
Meisner, Sanford, 16, 41
Meyerhold, Vsevolod, 1
Miller, Arthur, 74
Moon for the Misbegotten, A (O'Neill),
  57
Morley, Sheridan, 23
Mosher, Gregory, 16, 38, 80, 106

Nabokov, Vladimir, 120
National Public Radio, 20, 70
Neighborhood Playhouse, 4, 16, 41

Nelson, Jeanne-Andrée, 129 n. 40
Némath, Lenke, 95
November, 10
Nussbaum, Mike, 82

Old Neighborhood, The, 8, 9, 30–31,
  44, 59, 61
Old Religion, The, 8, 108, 113–19,
  120; anti-Semitism in, 117; Gematria
  in, 118; historical source of, 113–15,
  118–19; internal monologue in, 115,
  116; Mamet on race hatred in, 115
Oleanna, 8, 10, 14, 26, 31, 44, 64, 89,
  93–100; Asperger's traits in, 97–99;
  epigraphs of, 93–94; film adaptation
  of, 99, 100; lack of empathy in,
  97–98; Mamet on meaning of title,
  93; Mamet's direction of, 97; power
  and language in, 94–96; response to,
  97; tragedy in, 100
On Directing Film, 11
Organic Theatre, 4
Orton, Joe, 33
O'Neill, Eugene, 57

Pale Fire, 120
Penn, Sean, 8
Phagan, Mary, 113–16
Pidgeon, Rebecca (wife), 2, 8, 9, 16; in
  Oleanna, 97, 99
Piette, Alain, 26
Pinter, Harold, 27, 130 n. 13
Pope, Alexander, 120
Postman Always Rings Twice, The, 6
Pou, Charles, 131 n. 11
Powers, Francis Gary, 67
Prairie du Chien, 7, 22, 44
Psychiatric Dictionary, 98

Race, 10
Radavich, David, 22, 42, 47
"Rake, The," 3, 9, 14, 59
Rattigan, Terrence, 2
Redbelt, 8
Reunion, 5, 59–61
*Revenge of the Space Pandas or Binky
  Rudich,* 5
Rose, Charlie, 115

Rosser, Luther, 118
Roudané, Matthew, 72, 90

St. Nicholas Theater Company, 4;
    Mamet's resignation from, 5
Sanctity of Marriage, The, 44
Schachter, Steven, 4
Schenck, Joseph M., 98
Second City, 4, 22; influence on Sexual
    Perversity in Chicago, 45
Sedgewick, Eve Kosofsky, 47
Seeger, Pete, 130 n. 10
"Sex Camp," 4
Sexual Perversity in Chicago, 1, 4–6,
    44–52, 55, 58; charges of misogyny
    against, 51–52; homosexuality in, 47;
    sexual identity in, 48; treatment of
    misogyny in, 49;
Shawl, The, 7, 32, 69, 80–82, 88; Lind-
    say Crouse on, 81; Mamet on, 82;
Simon Suggs, 69
"Six Hours of Perfect Poker," 13
Skeele, David, 46
Slap Shot, 5
Slaton, John, 114
Smith, Adam, 72
Stafford, Tony, 129 n. 40
Society of American Theatre Critics, 6
Some Freaks, 11, 17
Souls of Black Folk, The (Dubois), 117
Sound of Music, The (Rodgers and
    Hammerstein), 5
South of the Northeast Kingdom, 11, 18
Sowell, Thomas, 10, 20
Spanish Prisoner, The (film), 8, 69, 113
Spanish Prisoner, The (play), 80
Speed-the-Plow, 7, 8, 10, 70, 83–88, 90;
    ending of, 87; Madonna in, 84
Squirrels, 26, 37–41; mentor relation-
    ship in, 39
Stanislavsky, Constantin, 1, 16
State and Main (Crouse and Lindsay),
    5, 8, 9
State of the Union (Crouse and Lind-
    say), 5
Steele, Shelby, 20
Stinton, Colin, 8, 51

Tested on Orphans, 10
Theatre, 11
Theory of the Leisure Class, The, 72
Three Sisters (Chekhov), 7
Three Uses of the Knife: On the Nature
    and Purpose of Drama, 11, 16, 17
"To Build a Fire," 111
Tolstoy, Leo, 1
True and False: Heresy and Common
    Sense for the Actor, 11, 16
"True Stories of Bitches," 13, 14, 96
Tuttle, Jon, 76, 101
Two-Speed Clock, The, 5

Uncle Vanya (Chekhov), 7
Unit, The, 3, 8, 10
Untouchables, The, 7

Veblen, Thorstein, 1, 72, 90, 93, 101
Verdict, The, 5, 6
Village, The, 5, 108, 109–13;
    depiction of emotions in, 112; ending
    of, 113; Hemingway's influence on,
    109–10, 111; hunting in, 111;
    imagery in, 110
Vint, 7
Voltaire , 46
Vorlicky, Robert, 74

"Wabash Avenue," 67
"Watch, The," 9
Water Engine, The, 5, 70–72, 88, 90,
    101; chain letter in, 71, 72
Way of All Flesh, The (Butler), 94
We're No Angels, 7, 8
White, Sanford, 71
"Why I Am No Longer a Brain-Dead
    Liberal," 10, 20; response to, 20
Wicked Son: Anti-Semitism, Self Hatred
    and the Jews, The , 10, 11, 18, 20;
    critical response to, 19
Wilde, Oscar, 10, 31–34
Williams, Tennessee, 16, 25, 62, 63
Wilson, Edith, 120
Wilson, Woodrow, 120
Wilson: A Consideration of the Sources,
    2, 10, 108, 120–22; critical response

to, 120; parody in, 120–21; puzzles and cryptograms in, 122
Winer, Linda, 54
Winslow Boy, The, 2, 8
Woods, The, 5, 6, 44, 45, 52–58, 64; fairy-tale motifs in, 56–57; Mamet on theme of, 58; psychological themes in, 56; symbolism in 54–55

Worster, David, 74
Woyzeck (Büchner), 101
Writing in Restaurants, 11–13, 69

Zinman, Toby, 100
Zweigler, Mark, 22